HERO OF MODERN TURKEY
ATATÜRK

BORN: 1881
DIED: November 10, 1938

When Mustafa Kemal was born, Turkey was weak and riddled with corruption. He gained a reputation as a brilliant young military officer, and in the chaotic aftermath of World War I rallied his people and won amazing victories on the battlefield and at the conference table. As first President of his creation, the Turkish Republic, he instituted reforms that revolutionized every aspect of Turkish life. Mustafa Kemal was arrogant and ruthless, but his singleminded dedication to his country earned him the name *Atatürk*—Father of Turkey.

Hero of Modern Turkey
Atatürk

By DEANE FONS HELLER

Julian Messner  New York

Published by Julian Messner
a division of Simon & Schuster, Inc.
1 West 39th Street, New York, N.Y. 10018
All Rights Reserved

Library of Congress Cataloging in Publication Data

Heller, Deane Fons, 1924–
    Hero of Modern Turkey: Atatürk.

    SUMMARY: A biography of the first President of the Turkish
Republic whose instituted reforms revolutionized every aspect of
Turkish life.
    Bibliography: p. 184
    1. Atatürk, Kamâl, Pres. Turkey, d. 1938.
    2. Turkey—History—1918-1960. [1. Atatürk, Kamâl, Pres. Tur-
key, d. 1938. 2. Turkey—History—1918-1960. 3. Turkey—Presi-
dents] I. Title.
DR592.K4H43   956.1'02'0924   [B] [92] 70-176379
ISBN 0-671-32541-8
ISBN 0-671-32542-6 (MCE)

Printed in the United States of America

CONTENTS

1
The Fallen Hero

On the evening of November 19, 1938, the body of Mustafa Kemal Atatürk, encased in an ebony casket drawn on a heavy gun carriage and flanked by twelve generals of the air, sea and land forces of the Republic of Turkey, left the ornate magnificence of the sprawling Dolma Boche Palace in Istanbul for its final resting place.

The great Mustafa Kemal, Father of Modern Turkey, would no longer guide the destiny of his people.

"Ata, Ata" ("Father"), the young and the old murmured in reverence as the procession moved along the wide Meclisi Mebusan Cadessi boulevard that skirts the western side of the Bosporus Straits and slowly made its way to the Galata Bridge that spans Istanbul's famed Golden Horn harbor.

The processional music, as the funeral cortege passed,

7

was the unfamiliar strains of Chopin's "March," rather than traditional Turkish music. Even in death, the great Turkish hero forced his people to accept and listen to Western music.

For a millennium, conquerors and heroes had passed this way. Xerxes, the ancient King of Kings of the Persians, built the first bridge across the straits as he led his armies in the ill-fated invasion of Greece. Alexander, too, had passed this way on his route of conquest of the then known world of Asia. Now Atatürk's final journey carried him across the teaming harbor while the last flickering blues and golds of the western Turkish sky reflected the gleam of swords of the soldiers in the procession.

The water vendors on the bridge refrained from calling out their familiar cry, "Su" ("water") to those who stood on the crowded, historic bridge. Beneath the bridge the numerous fish vendors stood silently on their gently bobbing boats, many with tears streaming down their care-worn faces. All were silent for that brief moment as the body of modern Turkey's creator passed by. All on the bridge were held frozen in grief. They could only stand and wait and hope for the future.

Who was this man, Mustafa Kemal Atatürk, and what did his loss signify to the Turks and Turkey's future?

"Much, very much," most Turks and many Westerners standing there on the bridge would have replied to such a question.

8

For Atatürk had almost singlehandedly wrested a modern Turkish republic out of the dying embers of a ruined Ottoman regime which had ruled—or, rather, misruled—the entire Middle East for centuries.

And he had done it against incredible odds following World War I, when Ottoman Turkey had emerged a beaten, broken empire, its borders insecure, its lands divided among the victorious allies who had won the war.

It was Atatürk who had raised the cry of rebellion, who had called his fellow Turks to arms and rallied them into resistance against their government and the allies.

"Turkey for the Turks" had been his battle cry.

And his fellow Turks had responded. They had joined his rebel "army," and together they had ousted the puppet Ottoman sultan, thrown the allies' armies out of Turkey's defeated, stricken capital city, Constantinople, and gone on to secure Turkey's borders.

Atatürk, who had worked tirelessly all his life to define Turkish soil and Turkish borders, had successfully created a nation within the brief span of his lifetime.

He had become a leader and a legend in his own time. When he died that tragic day, November 10, 1938, it signaled the passing of one of the most influential men the Middle East had ever known.

Even the Western representatives of governments long hostile to the Atatürk rebellion would eulogize him.

Said the British delegate at his funeral: "No other statesman of this age has surpassed Mustafa Kemal Atatürk."

It echoed the sentiment of others. The French government's delegate to his funeral called him "an awakener of the people."

Atatürk had swept away the crumbling facade of the old Ottoman Empire and substituted a government of the people of his native land. He had wrenched Turkey out of the Middle Ages, where she had slumbered so long. He had been, as his Turkish compatriots expressed it, "our teacher, our great chief."

In a special session of the Grand National Assembly, Atatürk was given a new title following his death. The Assemblymen conferred on him the name Ebedi Sef ("Eternal Chief"), in solemn gratitude for his lifetime efforts for Turkey.

What had been the Turkey of the Ottoman Empire into which this extraordinary man had been born?

Ottoman Turkey and the modern Turkey of Atatürk were and are vastly different places. Before World War I, Turkey was a sprawling, unwieldy territory which extended across the Arab world and embraced many diverse, non-Turkish peoples. At the height of its power, under the Sultan conquerors, the empire had in fact included all of North Africa, the Balkans and a wide sweep of land into Europe's heart.

The Ottoman Turks had entered Anatolia (in Asia

Minor) from the Asian steppes to the East in the thirteenth century, under the Nomadic leader Ertogrul Bey. They had found a strangely divided world held in part by the last faltering remnants of leadership of the Holy Roman Empire under the rule of the Byzantine Greeks and in part by the ruthless Seljuk Turks, who had come to plunder and conquer the land two centuries before.

The Ottoman Turks became a unified and formidable force under the leadership of Ertogrul's son, Osman, from whom the dynasty took its name—Osmanli, or Ottoman.

Osman, a vigorous fighting man of the almost treeless, windy Anatolian plains, expanded his holdings and became the first Sultan of the first Turkish Empire.

He and his warrior bands—they were little more than that in those early years of Empire—even gained Turkey's first toehold in Europe when they crossed the coveted Dardanelles and seized the Gallipoli peninsula.

It was Osman who organized what became the most disciplined and feared fighting force in the world, the famed Janizaries corps.

The Janizaries, at first recruited by force from subject Christian slaves, became Turkey's most elite military class and in time made up the noblest of Turkish families. By 1453 the Ottoman Sultans and their fearless war machine, the Janizaries, had captured the seat of Christendom—Constantinople. They then swept onward into the Balkans, crushing all in their path.

Later Sultans pushed the Empire's frontiers both

eastward and westward. In 1529, under Suleiman the Magnificent, the Turks threatened Vienna. But Vienna rallied and held.

The Turks besieged Vienna again in 1683 with an even stronger force. The fate of Europe may have hung in the balance that year. But terrified European monarchs, temporarily forgetting their petty quarrels, banded together and repulsed the assault.

By the sixteenth century, the Turkish Empire was the most formidable power on earth and its vast territories straddled three continents. But the tide of Turkish conquest ended at Vienna. The Turkish armies staggered and fell under the steady, united blows from the Russian, Austrian and Spanish allies. The Ottoman Empire had reached its zenith, and the long, painful and often bloody territorial retreat began—back to Asia Minor, where it had started.

By 1900 Turkey had become what Europe sarcastically called the "Sick Man of Europe." The Turkish sultanate was already stripped of meaningful power. Its government was a pawn, corrupt and outmoded, kept alive only for the convenience of the great European powers.

The Europe which the Turks had once held captive with fear had emerged the victor. It had become fiercely nationalistic and economically strong, while the Turkish government had become lifeless and obsolete. All internal Turkish power was still in the autocratic hands of the Sultan, who, in addition to his feeble state role, maintained absolute control over his Moslem subjects as the highest religious leader in all Islam, Defender of the Faith and Shadow of God on Earth.

To ensure the inviability of the Sultan in power, it had long been the royal custom that all male heirs to the Osmanli throne be killed on the accession of a new Sultan. (The royal heirs were customarily delicately strangled with silken cords so that no precious royal blood would flow.) Later, after 1700, this brutal custom was discontinued, and an orderly succession was arranged in which the oldest Osmanli heir automatically became Sultan. But a curious custom to keep Palace intrigue to a minimum was instituted. All other male heirs to the throne were shut up in the harem, the women's quarters of the ruling Sultan, and allowed little or no education and contact with the outside world. As a result, when the turn came for the accession of a new sultan, he was frequently found to be totally unfit to rule.

One exception was Sultan Mahmud II, who came to power in 1808. He immediately began to rebuild Turkey's by then discredited military force. It was Mahmud who first introduced modern weapons to his countrymen. With these he was able, finally, to extinguish the corrupt power of the now effete ruling Janizaries, whose tentacles of power pervaded all Turkish life.

It took Mahmud eighteen years to destroy the Janizaries. When a last-ditch remnant of the once famed and fierce corps rebelled in their barracks, Mahmud rolled up his newfangled cannon, fired repeatedly into the ranks of the mutineers and destroyed them. The fabled band was no more.

This bold but enlightened Sultan kept the feeble Ottoman state alive. He began many reforms to bring Turkey out of her ages-old stupor. He personally donned Western dress and urged his courtiers to follow suit. He abolished the turban in favor of the rakish wine-red fez—which in turn would be abolished under the twentieth-century reforms of Atatürk.

Mahmud established the country's first constitution and abolished the theory of absolute rule of the Sultan. Mahmud's efforts at Westernization, however, failed to stop the continuing dismemberment of the weakened Empire. One after the other, the people of the Balkan states—the Greeks, the Serbians, the Rumanians and the Bulgarians—rose up after centuries of repression and gained their freedom. The Western great powers—Russia, France and England—joined in the scramble. All gained sizable chunks of the Empire in the process.

No longer could the massive Black Sea be called a Turkish lake. Even the Islamic tribesmen across the North African coast seethed with revolt. But in spite of the disarray, the Ottoman regime staggered wobbly onward towards the twentieth century.

However, in 1876, five years before the birth of Atatürk, the short-lived liberalization of Turkish life ceased entirely. Abdul-Hamid came to the throne of the

Sublime Porte, as the Istanbul-based Sultanate palace was called.

This ruthless, backward-looking, ill-educated Sultan abolished the Constitution and savagely struck down the new and few civil liberties of his subjects.

Once again, Turkish life returned to the repressive stagnation of the past.

2

They Called Him Perfection

It was into this ruined, bankrupt world of unrest, lost empire and shattered fortunes that young Mustafa was born in 1881.

He was a Macedonian by birth and, though a Turk, was fair-skinned, blond and blue-eyed—an inheritance from his mother, Zubeyde, whose peasant ancestry came from a confusion of people in the western mountains of the Ottoman Empire, in the region which today is Albania.

His father, too, of whom little is known, came from the western mountains. Ali Riza was at first a minor clerk in the service of the government. He later attempted a trade in the lumber business but, being equally unsuccessful at that, drifted into what occupations he could find before his untimely death while Mustafa was still a young child.

As a result, the family of three, including Mustafa's sister, Makboula, lived in a rude shack in a poor section of Salonika, a teeming port city in Turkey's Rumeli (Turkey in Europe).

From this home—if the crude hut of dried mud could be called a home—Mustafa could see the shaggy heights of the mountains that surround the port.

The people, for all their poverty, their inadequate diet and the ugly, ill-designed hovels that served as homes, could draw a sustenance and spirit of independence from those mountains within the shadow of the lofty Mount Olympus itself, something denied them in the crowded, rat-infested city that clung to the hills along the sea.

And this the fiercely proud young Mustafa did, for while Macedonia, in the early years of his life, was a dying, drifting, decaying world under the weak rule of the Ottomans, legends bespoke her former glories.

Not far from Mustafa's birthplace lay ancient Pella. Here another blond, blue-eyed leader of men had been born—Alexander the Great. He had set his eyes on a pan-Hellenic world to the East and in his lifetime changed the fate of nations. Under the greatest of the Ottomans, the Turks had set forth. Marching across the top of Africa, they had conquered wherever they went. They had marched west into Europe, too, and forged their empire as far as Vienna.

The youthful, sullen, antagonistically proud Mustafa must certainly have pondered on the sad fate of Turkey's

17

glorious past. He might have dreamed, even then, of a possible future for his homeland full of hope and new glory.

All this was far off. Young Mustafa resented his life, and intensely disliked his poor, ill-fitting, peasant-style clothes, consisting of baggy trousers and a bloused shirt and sash, which set him apart from the more prosperous people of the city.

"When will I ever grow up and be someone?" he questioned himself as he sat cross-legged on the tattered rugs of his schoolroom floor.

He disliked intensely, too, the school he was required to attend, ruled by a hoja, or religious holy man . . . it was a school for poor Turkish boys. The teachings were based on the words of the Koran—the Moslem holy book.

Sprawled out on the floor about him were other Turkish boys—Jusuph, Musa and Yaha—all of whom lived in the same ghetto area of the city that he did.

Mustafa unhappily pondered on his world as he steathily ran a slender, bony hand down into the deep pockets of his trousers and brought out a fig. He lifted his eyes quickly to observe the hoja, who fortunately hadn't noticed and continued to drone on from his elaborate Arabic-script holy book.

Mustafa's special friend, Yaha, licked his lips but dared not ask for any of Mustafa's figs. If a boy showed a lack of attention while the hoja read, he would soon feel the sting of the hoja's cane across his back.

Mustafa seemed unconcerned as he looked unseeingly

through the open door, his tongue exploring the bit of fruit.

From where he sat he could gaze down upon the port, piled against the cliffs above the deep-blue Aegean Sea. While he hated his ghettolike world in this worldly port city, his mind responded to the city with its mixed populations.

From the open door he could see a part of the Seven Towers, a ruined fort on the lip of the sea below, and his bright eyes would record the round scallop of a nearby mosque with the needle sharpness of a graceful minaret rising above it.

But Mustafa, for all his daydreaming, kept his ear tuned to the hoja despite the fact that he found the lesson dull.

After all, his widowed mother, Zubeyde, desired that he attend. And she, a good Moslem, prostrated herself five times a day in prayer to ask Allah to raise the lowly station of her only son.

A tender look touched Mustafa's face as he thought of his mother.

But then his thoughts changed, and he leaned impishly over to whisper in his friend Yaha's ear, "What are you dreaming of? Will you make a good holy man and teach the Moslem religion, too?"

Yaha jerked away. "Why do you bother me?" he whispered back, not wanting to be caught by the hoja.

"I was thinking of sweet cakes," he added.

But Mustafa had lost interest in trying to divert his

friend from his lessons and merely muttered to himself, "I believe it is not the will of Allah that I serve Mohammed, the Prophet!"

Later, the shadows of the mountains fingered the hillside. This meant that school would soon close for the day.

Mustafa glanced longingly at the clear waters of the harbor, splashed with the movements of multishaped boats with brightly colored sails. He felt that now, at the age of twelve, he teetered on the brink of history, of great happenings. If he were only a man.

As the boys scurried away from the schoolroom adjacent to the mosque, they spotted a white-turbaned Moslem elder slowly making his way to the minaret alongside the mosque. Then, the high, nasal cry of this mussein penetrated the air as he called out evening prayer.

But Mustafa and his school friends ignored it and scuffled along to the poorer section of the town where their homes were, as other pedestrians glanced at the straight-limbed, blond lad racing along beside his dark complexioned schoolmates.

"How I hate it all!" Mustafa exclaimed as he kicked a small stone before him. "And tomorrow it will be the same. I'm tired of the sacred words of the Koran," he whispered hoarsely, half under his breath.

Yaha, Mustafa's friend, peered at him. He was accustomed to Mustafa's complaints—but this was blasphemy.

Didn't the Sultan-Caliph insist that Turkish boys be good Moslems and know their Koran?

And wasn't he the Shadow of God on Earth, as the hoja said?

Yaha sighed. Only yesterday the teacher had beaten him for inattention. Yet the intent face of his friend continued to smolder as they walked along the cobblestone streets.

"Yes," Yaha mused, "Mustafa is different. But he is a good friend, and somehow I feel proud to know him."

And with that he offered his friend a hazelnut from the small hoard in his pocket.

After Yaha left, Mustafa's unrest continued to hang in the air about him as a gentle south breeze off the harbor caressed his forehead and rumpled his hair.

His unrest seemed part of the deeper disharmony that hung over Macedonia. Already the alert Mustafa was aware of the rumblings among the Christian subjects of the city, who were attempting to free themselves from their Moslem overlords.

But despite encouragement from their neighboring Balkan countrymen and the smuggled nationalistic pamphlets coming into the city, the time was not yet ripe for action, for the Sultan's spies were everywhere.

Mustafa sighed again as he thought of the hatred with which he, a Turk, was held in this city, his birthplace, by his Christian neighbors, and how apart from them he really was.

And he thought of the morrow and how he would

21

once more be led in pious procession by the hoja as they made their way from the mosque to the schoolroom.

He suddenly took a violent dislike to the fact that he and his fellow Turkish students were required to sit on the floor and write their exacting lessons on their knees. The Christian children did not sit in that fashion in their schools. They sat erect in chairs at desks in lighted rooms.

He looked with disdain at the notebook in his hands with the exacting calligraphy lessons in the ornate Arabic script in which Turkish was printed as he slowly turned toward the door of his home.

The next day young Mustafa, who had been brooding all night, got up during his lessons. When he was ordered to reseat himself in the old manner, he defiantly refused.

"You dare to disobey me?" his teacher said ominously as he rose and pointed his willowy reed cane at Mustafa.

"Yes," said the boy, who accepted the blows that rained down upon him and then walked out of the classroom before the astonished eyes of the hoja and his school chums.

The proud and resentful Mustafa left the school, never to return.

It was a turning point in his young life. The beating by the hoja had only added to his defiance and instilled within him an even deeper dislike and scorn for the practices, superstitions and backward ways of the holy men who taught Turkish boys.

After a stormy session with his mother, who saw

clearly that young Mustafa was a precocious child, he won her over to his point of view.

"It's not for me, Mother, it's not for me," he had cried out with anguished sincerity.

"No, son, perhaps your place is elsewhere," she said softly, because his arguments had moved her strangely.

The next day she consulted with members of the family about where this discontented but brilliant young son of hers might find a place.

And it was decided that Zubeyde would take the two children to live in the country on a farm, managed by her brother, Hussein.

The freedom of the wild countryside gave Mustafa an opportunity to wander in solitude among the craggy hills, freed from the ill-smelling, zigzag streets of the Moslem quarter of the city.

The lonely wandering, with only a flock of sheep for companions, was good for Mustafa. Alone he could commune with nature and dream the dreams that adventures are made of.

"Ben olecegin" ("I am a Turk"), he would mutter fiercely to himself.

Or, carried away with the visions of grandeur to come and with the deeds of valor to be performed, he could shout it out against the treeless hills, startling his flock of bleating sheep grazing on the short, stubby grasses.

"Ben olecegin," he would shout.

In this harsh and rugged mountainous land, whose people were hardened and disciplined from centuries of wresting a living from the poor soil, his young body grew strong.

—In the country, Mustafa attended school intermittently. He alternated between attendance at a school under a Greek priest and the coaching of a tutor in the region. Neither masters were successful in challenging his eager mind.

He finally told his mother that the men were ignorant and he would no longer attend their lessons.

Zubeyde could only sigh sadly.

She knew her son's stubborn will, yet she was aware that he was destined for higher things than tending sheep. She decided that the family would return to the city and Mustafa would enroll in the new school there so that he might continue his education.

On their return, he obediently enrolled in the school his mother had selected, the Semsi Efendi, the first modern Turkish school in Salonika. It was one of a few such schools in the Empire—secular rather than under a Moslem holy man.

Mustafa was a good student. He insisted on adopting Western-style clothes and discarding the wide trousers and cummerbund typical of the Turkish schoolboy of the era.

For the first time, he was given lessons in the sciences and mathematics. He found the latter particularly stimulating and exciting. But secretly, perhaps encouraged by the remembrances of the grandeur of the Alexander myths he loved, he had decided he would become a soldier. With the aid of a friend's father, a Turkish officer in the Ottoman Army, he secretly took the entrance examinations to the Military Secondary School in Salonika and was accepted.

When his mother learned of his plan, she at first objected furiously, but finally bowed to his wishes.

"Kismet" ("Fate"), she would say as she knelt at nightly prayer.

Mustafa reminded his mother that, when he had been born, his father had hung a sword over his cradle and that meant for him to be a soldier.

"I was born a soldier. I shall die a soldier," he said with a determination unusual in a twelve-year-old boy.

The Turkish military schools were democratic institutions, and all students were admitted on the basis of scholarship alone. From the graduated officers the elite of the Turkish state was drawn. Boys from the middle classes, such as Mustafa, and from the peasantry could rise or fall in the Turkish society on the basis of their ability.

Instruction in the schools was fairly well rounded. Economics, history, philosophy and even Western literature were studied, as well as military science.

Mathematics was Mustafa's favorite subject. His teacher, a man also named Mustafa, was impressed with his mind and bestowed a second name on the young man—Kemal, which in Turkish means "excellent" or "perfection."

"My boy, your name is Mustafa, and so is mine. We

shall change this," the schoolmaster said. "From now on your name will be Mustafa Kemal."

It was a name he would retain all his life.

While in school, young Mustafa Kemal reveled and strutted about in the handsome Turkish uniform he was allowed to wear. He worked hard at the military school and at fourteen was advanced to the next-level officer's training course at Monastir, inland from Salonika, in the interior plains near the Greek and Albanian border of Turkey (now the town of Bitolj, in Yugoslavia).

Here Mustafa developed an enjoyment of poetry and worked diligently to perfect his reading and speaking ability in the French language.

Here, too, fact and far-off legends were further impressed on his mind. For 155 years after the death of Alexander, his empire was splintered among rivals at a battle fought on these broad Macedonian plains.

It was here at Monastir, while still in his teens, that a fierce patriotism flowered in young Mustafa Kemal, for the school was situated in a territory of the weakened Turkish Empire where there was constant strife between neighboring Greeks and Serbs to regain Macedonia.

Macedonia was, and is, a place full of different and contrasting national elements. The conglomerate population of Turks, Serbs, Moslem Slavs, Albanians, Bulgarians, Valachs, Greeks and Jews had been conquered by the Turks centuries before. They all detested the Sultan's rule.

Young Mustafa was exposed to the idea of nationalism here in the heart of the Balkans. The nationalistic flames of the West burned fiercely among these subjected people. They wanted to be free and set up their own governments.

Mustafa, a perceptive young man, learned the real nature of his own government's inefficiency. Corruption ran riot. Public officials extorted *baksheesh,* or graft, in the name of the Sultan to make a living. There was really no nation as such and no consistent policy toward the subject peoples of the Turkish Empire, whose loyalty to the Sultan-Caliph was imposed by terror.

During Mustafa Kemal's years at Monastir, the Greeks launched a war of liberation in Crete and the Turks marched against the Greeks in Rumeli. As the volunteers poured into the strategically located border town of Monastir, the boys from the military school, fired by the heroic epics and songs of the Ottoman conquests in Macedonia, attempted to join the troops leaving for battle.

Mustafa Kemal and a comrade stole out of their barracks one night and attempted to volunteer, but to no avail. They were refused and returned to their school.

His headmaster summed up the young, headstrong cadet as "a brilliant but difficult youth."

Mustafa Kemal's new awareness of the politics of the state and the conflicting patriotism that bred of wars of liberation were to prove an important part of his education as an officer of the Empire and a future leader of his people.

At the outpost town of Monastir, Mustafa Kemal met Ali Fethi, a Macedonian like himself, but far more urbane. Through the charming, cosmopolitan Fethi, young Mustafa Kemal was introduced to the heady world of the French philosophers, whose political ideas and conscience had flamed the fires of rebellion against tyranny late in the eighteenth century. Voltaire, Rousseau and Montesquieu were a few of these liberal political thinkers to whom he was exposed. The young Mustafa Kemal worked diligently at his faulty French so that he could truly savor their ideas more readily.

The two young cadets eagerly discussed the radical ideas of man's basic right of individual freedom without despotism imposed by a tyranical governing class, such as the Sultanate-Caliphate of Turkey imposed on its people.

Mustafa Kemal formed one other close friendship at the Monastir school—that with sensitive young Omer Naji, who introduced him to the beauty and delights of poetry. But, despite these two friendships, young Mustafa Kemal continued to remain aloof from most of his fellow cadets. This preference to be alone would remain with him all his life.

His headmaster would later remember him with these words: "It is impossible to be intimate with him."

Mustafa Kemal's ambition and thirst for glory had already taken root.

"I am going to be somebody," he was heard to have remarked.

In the final year of the nineteenth century, young Mustafa Kemal was graduated from the Senior Military School at Monastir as a second lieutenant in His Majesty, the Sultan's Army. Because of his brilliant record at the school, he was immediately admitted to the Sultan's highest military school, the General Staff War College at Harbiye in Constantinople.

3

Young Officer Days

"Halt! Who goes there?"

"Second Lieutenant Mustafa Kemal, sir." And with that he executed a smart salute as he reported for duty in Constantinople.

Determined to be a good soldier, he studied furiously and for long hours, even after his fellow officer students had gone to bed in the barracks they shared at the War College.

But Friday, the holy day, was free, and then he took to exploring the city around him.

To the spruce, eighteen-year-old, provincially educated Mustafa Kemal, the city was exciting. Sometimes he felt as though he could not get enough of it.

Unable to turn his eyes and ears away from the sights and sounds of the great seaport, crossroads of the world,

he often stayed out until morning, when he had to report for classes.

Constantinople is and was a heady experience.

Its wonders spill out, offering all the cosmopolitan delights of a capital city with a long and fascinating history as the last true bastion of the Holy Roman Empire after Rome itself had fallen.

Although the Moslem conquest of the city in 1453 had changed the religion as well as the outlook of the handsome old city, the layers of old Byzantium could still readily be seen.

In the bazaars one could enter huge vaulted rooms where the Emperor Constantine had stabled the Imperial horses.

In the vast museums of the Sultan were treasures untold, including a huge marble sarcophagus of Alexander the Great, one of several ordered by that ancient monarch. On the tree-lined boulevard near Santa Sophia was a beautifully wrought obelisk that once graced Cleopatra's Egypt.

The youthful Mustafa drank of the beauty of history all around him.

And there was so much more. Constantinople is really three cities. It straddles two continents and the fabled Bosporus Straits, which flow swiftly between its old and new sections.

The sights, the sounds and the scents are a mixture of East and West—particularly from the Galata Bridge, the incredibly busy highway bridge across the Golden Horn

harbor which divides two of the three cities within European Constantinople, Pera and Old Stambul.

It was here on the Galata Bridge that two fellow officers caught up with Mustafa as he stopped to drink in the sights and listen to the water vendors and fish salesmen on their boats, swaying at anchor on the Stambul side of the harbor.

"Distractions! Give us more distractions," one of the dapper uniformed officers said as he smilingly slapped Mustafa's shoulder.

The young men lingered there beside Mustafa, smoking and feeling the rich fabric of Constantinople. They had frequented one of the cafés that was a favorite of Mustafa's, and their spirits were lifted from the heady raki they had been drinking.

They joked together, with their talk lingering upon the fleshpots of the brightly lighted, lively city, as the deep golds and purples of the setting sun descended over the mosques of Stambul, silhouetted against the western sky.

Mustafa, half listening, remained a little aloof until one of his companions turned to him and said, "Are you joining us?"

When he said he'd stay on the bridge a little longer, his companion shook his head and said, "Oh, never mind, Mustafa. You are the one who is always thinking. Thoughts appear to rise in your head like leavening in good Turkish bread."

These words sounded familiar to young Lieutenant

Mustafa Kemal and reminded him that an instructor at his senior military school had called him "brilliant but difficult."

Mustafa Kemal stayed behind as the other officers turned to wind their way into the bazaars of Stambul and explore its pleasures in the winding warren of twisting streets that made up that section of the city where the Moslem population lived.

Then he slapped his thigh with his glove and walked off rapidly toward Pera, the newer, brighter section of the city, where the foreign population resided.

As he walked along the quay he looked across the Bosporus and watched a ferry make its way to Constantinople's third city—Uskadar, on the Asian mainland.

Then he quickly jumped aboard one of the smaller ferryboats, manned by a wizened sailor whose weatherbeaten face seemed almost black in the dim light of early evening.

He would go to Uskudar and set foot on Asian soil for the first time.

As the boat slowly plied its way across the famous straits, Mustafa thought of the political unrest of the day, wondering to himself what role he would play in his country's future.

Quick in his perception as he looked out on the city, which seemed to surround him and his companions in the boat, he saw it for what it was—a city of pleasure. He decided that Constantinople, with its decadent mixtures of East and West, was not a city for the business of government of the Turks.

But the distractions of the city fascinated him. He particularly enjoyed roaming through the Europeanized city of Pera, with its bright lights and Western ways. Here the European colonies lived a life apart. The foreigners obeyed their own laws, not those of the Turkish authorities, and enjoyed a tax-free status under what was called Capitulations, which gave foreigners extra-territorial privileges. The Capitulations, detested by turn-of-the-century liberal Turks, who found themselves in somewhat of the position of second-class citizens in their homeland, had been granted by earlier Sultans when Turkey desperately needed foreign capital.

In this atmosphere, some of Mustafa Kemal's early conviction to be only a good, professional soldier slowly changed. And he admitted: "I was full of the dreams of youth. I neglected my lessons."

In the highly charged political atmosphere of the city, young Mustafa Kemal drank deeply of the knowledge and intrigues around him. Political thoughts and ambitions entered his simple soldier's life. The times were ripe for political fomentation, for these were the days of the repressive, autocratic reign of Sultan Abdul-Hamid II.

Secretly young Mustafa Kemal read the banned liberal writings of the Turkish patriot Namil Kemal. It is highly probable that he read French translations of works of Tolstoi, the Russian writer who transmitted so much of the enlightened thinking for emancipation of the Russian serfs at this time and, of course, more of the works of both Voltaire and Rousseau, the French writers who had given voice to freedom more than a century before. Finally, in 1902, at the age of twenty-three, Mustafa Kemal entered the elite professional ranks of soldiering and enrolled in the War Academy, the highest military school in the land. Here, too, he would admit to furthering his political knowledge.

"New ideas were coming to me and some of my friends," he said. "We began to discover that there were many bad things in the administration and political life of the country."

His new political awareness led him to join a small political organization. Among their goals was the printing and distribution of a small revolutionary newspaper.

"We were seized with enthusiasm to explain our discoveries to the thousands of students that made up the War Academy," he said in defense of his position as political agitator for much-needed reforms in the government of the Sultan.

"I was on the executive committee and wrote most of the articles in the newspaper," he confessed.

While he was in school, another organization, the committee of Union and Progress, was formed in his home city of Salonika. It was led by a Turkish officer named Enver, and would lead to the so-called Young Turks movement for reforms under a united Turkey with the Sultan still at its head. Mustafa, however, felt otherwise. He had become keenly aware of the weakness of the Empire, with its mixture of national and religious factions. He began to see the Sultan not as an instrument of the various power groups but as a real impediment to progress if Turkey was to become united and a nation.

"Turkey for the Turks" became the rallying cry of Mustafa Kemal and his friends.

"Turkey must be the fatherland instead of a despot unable to reconcile his policy with his people's interests," he said.

The young officers trying to educate their fellow classmates in a progessive, twentieth-century, Western approach to reforms enjoyed their clandestinely prepared newspaper adventure for only a short time. The school authorities soon found out about the activity and put a stop to it.

Fortunately, the director of the school, Piza Pasha, showed indulgence to the youthful plotters, and the punishment for their offense was merely detention in their rooms. Ironically, even among the older officers, the elite of the realm, there was much ill will toward the inequalities of the Sultanate, even if these feelings were not directed at the Sultan personally. In fact, the first revolutionary movement in the Empire had sprung up among student officers in the Imperial Military Medical School in 1889—fully a decade earlier. Their planned *coup d'état* against the government had ended in failure, and the leaders were rounded up and exiled to remote parts of the vast empire. But the revolutionary thoughts went on.

While plans of political reform whirled through Mustafa Kemal's ever-active mind, he thirsted for all the knowledge he could garner. Military science, tactics and problems of guerrilla warfare especially interested him— so much so that a chance but sage remark by an instructor in the War Academy that guerrilla war "is difficult to suppress as to wage" led him to eagerly pursue the subject. He threw himself into a thorough study of the matter and evolved a hypothetical problem of revolt to be waged against the capital at Constantinople from the Asian Anatolian vastness to the east.

It was almost as though Mustafa Kemal had already read his destiny and saw ahead to the not far distant day when he would lead such a people's revolt to save Turkey, and guerrilla warfare tactics would be required.

"Turkey for the Turks," which was to be his lifelong ambition for his beloved country, was crystallized and formalized in Constantinople at the turn of the century.

4

The Making of a
Professional Soldier

For a few months following his graduation from the War
Academy, the newly gazetted Captain Mustafa Kemal
found that he had much free time on his hands. He had
time for the revolutionary ideas that bubbled in his mind
and stirred him with hopes for being instrumental in
Turkey's future, and he and several officer friends, many
of whom had been at the War Academy with him and
had been active in the publication of the clandestine
newspaper urging reform, again drifted together.

Among the group was Ali Fuad, who, with his quick
wit and his love of poetry and books of philosophy, had
opened a new world of Western ideas to Mustafa.

The group met frequently in different places to dis-
cuss the political ideas which burned within them and
which they hoped to put into practice one day—soon—

and which might end the repressive, autocratic regime of Abdul-Hamid II.

Often they met in small cafés. While drinking their raki, a strong white liquid which was cheap and easy to obtain, or sipped at tiny cups of sweet black Turkish coffee, they talked far into the night.

This night, as Mustafa turned into a door where he heard the sinuous sounds of Oriental music and quickly located his fellow conspirators, he found them discussing the publication of a bulletin of ideas for revolt and reform.

They talked, too, of the enlightened thinking of Tolstoi and the inspiration for free thinking and action that Rousseau and Voltaire espoused, as their youthful minds soared with the lilting music and the sound of the clinking of their glasses.

"I like to chew up and digest everything they say," Mustafa would say with enthusiasm.

The Turkish secret police were aware of their meetings, for the Sultan's spies were everywhere, and they kept the young men under surveillance. But they did nothing, since the group seemed only to meet to talk.

When, however, they began to turn out their revolutionary pamphlets, the police acted. All of the young conspirators were arrested and detained for questioning.

While being held in the Sultan's notorious Red Prison, with its damp walls and poor food and sanitation, Mustafa spent most of his time reading books and writing verse.

Fortunately, his mother was able to come to Constantinople and was allowed to visit him and bring him food and books and papers during his stay in the squalid cell allotted to him.

Fortunately, too, Mustafa and Ali Fuad, who had both made superior records of scholarship at the War Academy, were pardoned quickly. The director of the War Academy interceded for these two bright, if imprudent, officers.

"Both have been graduated with high honors in their class," he said, pointing out that they were two of only thirteen in the entire school who had won staff officer positions in the Sultan's army, that year.

Both, however, were promptly shipped off to distant Syria, away from the intrigues of the capital, and placed on probation.

Syria, sparsely populated and mostly desert, seemed an unlikely place for either of them to plot any further subversive activities against the Sultanate.

Although it meant banishment from the mainstream of activity and political reform ideas, to Mustafa it meant more time for quiet study of how success might yet one day crown his efforts to gain the reform he knew Turkey must make to survive.

In Damascus, Syria, he again had much free time to read and write down some of his ideas. Here, too, he gained the disquieting knowledge of the inefficiency of the Sultan's government at first hand. All around him he could see the corruption of the officials and see at close hand the plight of the people, who were heavily taxed and cruelly exploited under the loosely supervised and feeble structure of the far-flung Ottoman Empire.

Graft was the order of the day. It pervaded all levels of the administration, including the Army.

Mustafa Kemal soon became aware that many of the Turkish units sent to control local tribesmen simply plundered their villages. These "raids," in which both the officers and the soldiers of the Sultan extracted gold or anything worth while, sowed seeds of hatred and revolt against the Turks among the villagers. This new, firsthand knowledge of the corruption in the Turkish regime, even down to the lowest ranks in the army, served to fire Mustafa Kemal's mind with the need of reform—and soon!

More than this, his new knowledge of the diverse peoples of the Empire, such as the backward Arab tribesmen in the deserts east of Damascus, led Mustafa Kemal to re-evaluate just how effective a government could be among such a polyglot population. His old theme of "Turkey for the Turks" soon had new and deeper meaning.

Perhaps the united, nationalistic Turkey he dreamed of would be better off without the peoples of the areas he saw.

Mustafa performed his more mundane military duties, such as teaching his brother officers the special skills he had gained at the War Academy, well. But he continued to agitate among them for the need of reform. He helped

41

organize a secret society, the Vatan ve Hurriyet ("Fatherland and Freedom"), to further the cause for a new Turkey. He worked quietly and discreetly so as not to arouse suspicion among the Sultan's spies.

Secretly, he longed to go back to Salonika, where the real work of revolution was practicable. With the help of one of his commandants in Damascus, he took a leave of absence from his post and spent some months in Macedonia. While there, he met with and arranged for a number of his former friends to meet and found the Macedonian Chapter of the Vatan movement. He dreamed and planned to further his destiny as Turkey's leader, though he returned to his post in Syria.

"I have ambitions, and even very great ones," he wrote to a friend. "However, they do not consist in material satisfactions like holding high places and gaining large sums of money.

"I seek the realization of these ambitions in the success of a great idea which, while profiting my country, will give me the keen satisfaction of a duty worthily accomplished."

In September, 1907, his promotion to adjutant major came through, and he was finally posted to the Third Army in Macedonia. Now he felt he could work in earnest toward his country's freedom from the repressive rule of the Sultan. Revolution was in the air in Macedonia, fanned by nationalistic breezes blowing from Europe among the peoples of the adjacent Balkan states.

However, Mustafa Kemal was destined not to take an

active or leading part in the momentous events of the following year. During his exile in Syria, the committee of Union and Progress, under the leadership of Enver, had grown in strength while the Vatan had not. His Vatan would eventually be swallowed up by the Committee, or Unionists, and lose its identity.

"The hour of deliverance arrived," he said later of the 1908 revolt, but he, somewhat bitterly, found himself pushed into the background as Enver took over the leadership of the movement which history would long remember as that of the Young Turks.

Once again he divorced himself, as much as he was able, from political affairs and plunged into military projects. The Committee leaders sent him on a diplomatic mission into North Africa—to Tripoli. It was as much a political maneuver to get him out of the way as a military or diplomatic necessity. Mustafa Kemal left, resignedly, for his post. This new exile and his despair at not being allowed to help direct the reforms the revolt aimed at must have mounted during these crucial months.

While he was again successfully performing his new duties, Mustafa Kemal's thoughts were back in Macedonia as he pondered where and what the Young Turks' revolution would actually mean for Turkey. He concluded that although the Sultan, Abdul-Hamid, had granted the desired Constitution which he had suspended a decade earlier, it was not enough.

"The windows of the Turkish edifice of state were

thrown open," he recalled years later in a famous speech to the Turkish National Assembly. "But the building itself remained the same."

Many accused Mustafa Kemal of being jealous of Enver's role in the revolutionary movement sweeping Turkey. When the Sultan betrayed the revolutionists, it was Enver who deposed him and set up his brother Mohammed, as Sultan. It was Enver, again, who received the praise and plaudits of the crowds.

"Naturally I'm jealous of him," Mustafa Kemal admitted to friends. Perhaps, though, he had every right to be bitter and complain, since he believed himself to have the greater capabilities as a leader of the new Turkey.

Actually, the Young Turks' Revolution under Enver had no real program of reform and no basic understanding of the "heart of the matter" as Mustafa Kemal saw it. His view was that the basic weakness of the structure was the Caliphate role of the Sultan, as the "shadow of God on earth." This created a religiously dominated Empire trying to reconcile a sprawling world of ethnically and religiously mixed peoples who were already caught up in the nationalistic fervor sweeping Europe and longed to be independent.

Mustafa Kemal's vision of reform differed from that of the others. He openly recognized that democracy of a popular sovereignty was impossible, because of a Caliphate based on Islamic religious law.

Mustafa felt that it was because of this that the country was held back. To him the religious domination of the state was at fault.

"Political reform meant religious reform. Islam, the religious basis of the government, would have to go!"

The Young Turks' Revolution contributed to the further disintegration of the Ottoman Empire, for forces were let loose that could not be stopped.

The Greeks took Crete, with its predominately Greek population. Italy entered the decaying Ottoman scene and invaded Tripolitania (now the independent Arab kingdom of Libya). Open warfare flared there as the weakened Ottoman forces desperately attempted to hold their North African possessions.

Mustafa Kemal was sent across Egypt to lead the campaign in Tripolitania, but the cause was lost before he arrived. He was able to rally his small forces and won one battle, but the war itself was short and disastrous for the Turks.

While Turkey, its back to the wall, was fighting to hold on to Tripolitania, the Balkans erupted. An obscure king, Nicholas—called Little Nicholas, of Montenegro, the Black Mountain kingdom to the north of Macedonia and Albania and today incorporated in modern Yugoslavia—declared war on Turkey on October 8, 1912. Bulgaria and Greece joined in, and the Balkans were aflame.

As Mustafa Kemal journeyed wearily back from Tripolitania after the Sultan had signed a peace treaty with victorious Italy, he learned of the fall of Monastir to the

Serbians and of his native Salonika in Macedonia to the Greeks. By the time he reached Constantinople, almost all of Rumeli (what the Turks called the European part of the Ottoman Empire) was lost save one small but significant and strategic area—the Gallipoli peninsula. It guards the Dardanelles (which the Turks call Chanak Kale Bogazi), the approaches to Constantinople itself, and the Bosporus Straits to the Black Sea.

Here Mustafa Kemal, who had already garnered a reputation as a brilliant commander, was sent.

It was a prophetic and fateful post, for Gallipoli would play a decisive role in Mustafa Kemal's destiny.

Mustafa Kemal's purely military role satisfied his needs and filled his days with action. But it left him clearly outside the mainstream of the Young Turks' reform programs for Turkey.

Already his thoughts were crystallizing as to the direction Turkey should take, and already he had become highly suspicious of the vague and inadequate measures Enver was taking. The idea of pan-Islamism and the reactionary and retarding influence of the Moslem religion on the everyday life of the Turks led him to espouse the growing concept that a sweeping secularization of the Empire was essential.

These thoughts were shared by many fellow members of the Union and Progress Party. Along with many of the more democratically thinking elements in the Party, he rejected the pan-Ottomanism that Enver and his Young Turk movement preached.

Mustafa Kemal's service in Syria had already led him to reject the belief that a real link between all Mohammedans in the Empire still existed. He considered these two Young Turk programs as unrealistic as Enver Pasha's aims of uniting all the Turkish tribes of Asia.

What he came to believe in instead was the concept of the Turkish national ideal and the development of a national conscience.

The revolt of 1908 and the Balkan Wars of 1910-12 had already fired Mustafa Kemal and many liberals such as himself to appreciate only one thing—the existence of the country as a whole and united "fatherland."

No longer could Mustafa Kemal look up to the Sultan —the old and ailing and totally unfit puppet, Mohammed V, installed by Enver as the country's nominal leader.

These were not the only differences he discovered which shook his confidence in the programs of Enver Pasha.

The nagging fear of the pro-German policies of the regime also tugged at his growing nationalism. The new Turkey he began to dream of should be free of foreign domination and free within her frontiers to develop as a true modern nation. This new Turkey should certainly not be wooing new and ambitious allies.

5

Gallipoli

In the summer of 1914, World War I exploded across the face of Europe. Although the clouds of war had long been festering, it was only after the assassination of the Austrian heir to the Hapsburg throne, Archduke Franz Ferdinand, by a Serbian terrorist group in the small Balkan city of Sarajevo that Europe's armies moved.

Unfortunately for Turkey, Enver's Committee Government, under Sultan Mohammed V, had already signed a secret pact with Germany's Kaiser Wilhelm which committed the Turks to a treaty of mutual alliance with the Germans in the conflict.

Despite the agreement, however, Turkey continued to maintain an outward neutrality. In reality, the issue was already joined. When, on August 11, the Sublime Porte permitted two belligerent German battleships, the

Goebin and the *Breslau,* to enter the Dardanelles and granted them refuge from a pursuing British warship, Turkey's entrance into the war was settled.

Enver then proceeded to officially "buy" the two German vessels and hired their crews to serve in the Ottoman Navy. He then dismissed the British admiral who had been serving the Sultan and replaced him with a German admiral serving on one of the ships. Then, in early October, the two ships, renamed the *Sultan Selim* and the *Medilli* but still manned by their German crews, steamed up the Bosporous Straits, entered the Black Sea and attacked the Russian fleet there.

The result was a declaration of war against the Turks by the Russians, followed by similar declarations by her Entente partners, England and France.

The young, newly promoted Lieutenant Colonel Mustafa Kemal, serving as a military attaché in Bulgaria at the time of Turkey's entrance into the war, was appalled.

He showed a remarkable grasp of international politics as he wrote his friends denouncing Turkey's role as a German puppet. He was certain that it would be a long and costly war and that Turkey should remain neutral and independent in the conflagration that was engulfing all Europe.

Others, including ministers in Enver's Committee Government, agreed.

"It will be our ruin," said Javid, an associate of Mustafa Kemal's from the early years of the Committee and Union and Progress in Salonika.

"The outcome of this war will not be certain for us or our allies," agreed Mustafa Kemal.

His soldier's instinct was alerted too. Logistically he felt that the stretching of the thin fabric of the Turkish Army across the wide frontier required was foolhardy.

"We declared mobilization without even determining our aims," he declared, and he cautioned: "It will be harmful for us to maintain a large army for a long period."

He was gloomily certain, too, that it would be a long, grim war.

To add to his gloom, there was the nagging doubt of the loyalty of the Ottoman subjects. Of the twenty-five million people in the Ottoman Empire, only ten million were Turks. Another ten million were Arabs, many of whom had made abortive attempts at freedom before. Mustafa Kemal seriously doubted that they could be relied on to defend the Empire. He was equally unconvinced of the loyalties of the other minorities—the Kurds, the Assyrians and the Armenians.

The German high command, who took over all Turkish forces, evolved a strategy which brought the Turks into battle against the Russians on her northeast border, the English on her southern frontiers and a French expeditionary force in the east.

"It was madness."

Germany also demanded that Turkey close the Straits, cut the Suez Canal and Aden and attack and invade Russia in the Caucasus in order to hold down Russian troops there and keep them from the European front.

The young Mustafa Kemal was ordered to the Gallipoli peninsula, to command the Nineteenth Division being formed there. Although the over-all commander was a very capable German general, Liman von Sanders, Mustafa left for the front with a heavy heart.

For him being posted to Gallipoli, however, was to be one of few fortunate decisions of the Enver government in the conduct of the ill-fated war.

Mustafa had studied the terrain during the disastrous Balkan War a few years earlier and knew it well. His advice to his superior, von Sanders—known to the Turks as Liman Pasha—on the defense of the area was based on the only firsthand intelligence available.

It would serve Turkey in good stead.

The Gallipoli peninsula campaign would be a decisive factor in saving Constantinople from falling to the Entente allies, and the battles waged there would earn Mustafa Kemal the adulation of the Turks so important to his destiny.

As he jabbed his pointer at von Sanders' maps, Mustafa Kemal informed the more mature and seasoned German general that certain defense measures would fail on the narrow beaches of Gallipoli.

"Here and here," he pointed out, would be where the invasion would come.

His experiences in the Tripolitania War, where the Italians had successfully landed their forces under naval bombardment of the African coast, had taught him that strictly land defenses of barbed wire on Gallipoli would be totally inadequate.

He quickly convinced the astute German commander that the British naval forces, so superior to any other naval forces of the time, would easily be able to land troops on the narrow jutting finger of land of the peninsula.

Gallipoli's beaches, with their steep ridges high above the Aegean waters that break against the shore, would be a prime target for British bombardment. It would mean the Turks would have to fight from the ridges.

Should the British succeed in landing an invasion force on Gallipoli, he pointed out, their allies, the Russians, would be able to get supplies from Europe and aid them in enveloping the Turkish positions from both the European and the Asian frontiers. For Gallipoli ran like an arrow into the heart of Turkey—Constantinople.

"It is essential that Gallipoli be held!" he almost shouted in his passionate defense plans of his homeland.

But how?

The entire Turkish high command was in complete disagreement as to battle strategy. Even Liman Pasha was convinced that the real attack would occur across the way on the Turkish Asian mainland and not on Gallipoli itself.

Despite Mustafa Kemal's eloquent appeal, the German officer decided to move the main Turkish army divisions there.

He did leave Mustafa Kemal stationed on the peninsula itself to command the Nineteenth Division—but only as a reserve unit which could be moved in any direction once the battle situation became clear, Liman Pasha emphasized.

Young Colonel Mustafa Kemal remained unconvinced. He was sure that the main attack would occur from the West and on the peninsula itself—not on the Asian mainland. He knew, almost instinctively and with that special perception of a superb strategist, that the area would have to be defended from the heights of the craggy cliffs above the beaches of Gallipoli.

So he staked his division and his reputation on this strategy with a bold and imaginative battle plan—and without authority.

As he hastily prepared for the coming invasion he marched the bulk of his reserve troops, without orders to do so, to the crest of the steep heights of Sari Bair at a place known as Chunuk Bair. It was here, he was convinced, that the invasion would occur.

Mustafa Kemal was brilliantly, if recklessly, playing his "hunches." Despite lack of information and the chaotic conditions of the battlefield amid the scrubby, boulder-strewn ascent, he knew, intuitively, that he and his men had to reach the crest of Sari Bair—and soon.

On that very night of April 25, in fact, the Allied forces of the British and French, with their Anzac troops (Australians and New Zealanders), did precisely what Mustafa Kemal believed they would do.

They landed at Cape Hellas, on the tip of Gallipoli, and slightly north of Gaba Tepe on the beach at Airburnu, on the western slope of the Sari Bair ridge. Simultaneously, the French landed a small, strictly diversionary force on the Asiatic mainland coast of Turkey, where the main Turkish forces lay in wait.

The suspense was intense as Mustafa Kemal waited. An officer finally reported to the anxious Mustafa Kemal that troops had been sighted coming toward Chunuk Bair.

"But it is not known whether the troops are the enemy's or ours," he added helplessly.

Mustafa Kemal rightly judged that the troops were the enemy!

The Anzac troops had indeed landed a large force on the beach at Airburnu. Since no adequate defenses had been prepared at that precise beachhead, the troops were already making their way up the western slope of Chunuk Bair, as Mustafa Kemal's forces struggled up the steep eastern cliffs to gain the same heights.

While his men rested briefly on one of the ridges beneath the crest, Colonel Kemal and a few staff officers went on ahead.

Suddenly a stream of Turkish soldiers, sent earlier as a lookout to the crest, came running toward him.

"The enemy, sir."

"They come," several in the lead shouted.

"Where?" demanded Mustafa.

At this the officer in charge pointed down the western

slope and for the first time Mustafa Kemal saw the enemy approaching.

It was a major assault force.

Colonel Kemal immediately ordered his forces to be sent for on the double and ordered the sentry advance group back to their post on the ridge.

Their ammunition was already spent, and Colonel Kemal ordered them to fix bayonets and lie on the ground across the entire ridge to hold back the first onslaught of the enemy.

"When our men lay down, the enemy lay down," he said afterward.

"And this was the necessary moment of time we gained."

That moment may have been decisive, for it gave his rear forces time to reach the crest. By midday, Mustafa Kemal's reckless race against time was won.

He had reached the ridge just in the nick of time and against tremendous odds, with only one incomplete division against a strong, heavily armed enemy force.

"I don't order you to attack; I order you to die," he shouted at his men.

Fighting alongside the men with unswerving energy and disregard for personal safety, he inspired his troops. His soldiers came to believe that he was favored by Allah and was under the protection of the Jinns—which, Turkish legends claimed, were the special guardians of the brave.

The idea that he was under the special protection of

the Jinns was further fostered when Mustafa Kemal received a direct hit during the battle. A shell splinter struck near his heart, but hit a heavy gold pocket watch he carried with him. He emerged unscathed.

"The ferocity of that battle can hardly be described," he explained later as he spoke of the acrid smell of smoke amidst the heather and scorching heat on the ridge that day on Chunuk Bair. "The smell of death and flies and scorpions was everywhere." "But they were Turkish scorpions," he said proudly.

According to one newspaper account, Mustafa Kemal, the hero of the moment, described the first battle of Gallipoli as almost exclusively hand-to-hand combat.

"When all the men in the first trench fell," he said, "the second line simply and automatically moved up to take their fallen comrades' places—even knowing they, too, would fall."

Mustafa Kemal's Turks, fighting on Turkish soil, indeed fought bravely that day. They earned the respect of an enemy British commander who later, in writing of the battle, praised them in these words: "It was the rare, fighting quality of the Osmanli soldier at work."

As for Mustafa Kemal, his military fame was assured that day when he and his men stood firm on that bleak, craggy ridge above the blue Aegean Sea.

Mustafa Kemal, soon to be promoted, had learned an important lesson in the art of war under fire. It was the importance of a single moment that often decides the fate of battle. And he would rely on that knowledge again and again in the fighting years ahead.

Despite the confidence gained and the battle won, there was still much to do, and the Turkish Army was ill prepared for the task. The army lacked proper food, clothing and even ammunition. The Turkish high command continued to be disunited, disagreeing as to future strategy to hold the area.

The enemy supplied by British warships in the sea below continued to grow stronger and held on doggedly to their toehold of beach at Airburnu. They sent wave after wave of well-armed troops up the steep ridges of Chunuk Bair. The Turks were virtually helpless, since they lacked the proper guns and necessary rounds of ammunition.

Ultimately, the enemy gained the ridge and forced the Turks back—but not before suffering enormous losses.

Mustafa Kemal pleaded with von Sanders for a unified command. Instinctively he knew that a massive enemy maneuver was building up. He firmly believed that it would again take place on the western side of Gallipoli, on the entire Sari Bair range above Chunuk Bair to Kija Chemin, and further north to the lofty heights of the Tekke Tepe, on the Anafarta Ridges of the mountain chain.

"The enemy must not take those heights," he insisted.

"There is one moment more," he added, and warned:

"If we lose that moment, we are faced with a general disaster."

In fact, catastrophe already threatened the entire front as the British warships and British troops poured in on the exhausted Turks.

Finally, in almost the eleventh hour, von Sanders gave the brash young Kemal the command he had asked for.

And again he acted with his usual audacity, and instinctive military tactics, against the advice of the earlier plans of his superior officers. Mustafa's assessment of the situation proved correct. The next and last major offensive came from the beaches at Airburnu, where the enemy landed twenty thousand fresh troops who again attempted to scale the ridges along a broad front—precisely where Mustafa expected them.

Another force of troops landed to the north to penetrate the Anafarta mountain range and attempt to cut the Turkish lines of communication.

"Control of those ridges," Mustafa rightly surmised, "would give the enemy the entire peninsula, the Dardanelles and the road to the heart of the Empire—Constantinople."

Winston Churchill, then the first Lord of the Admiralty in London, a major proponent of the plan to seize the Dardanelles, would say in recognition of the strategic importance of Gallipoli: "Through the narrows of the Dardanelles, and across the ridges of Gallipoli, lie some of the shortest paths to a triumphant peace."

But Mustafa Kemal, correctly second-guessing the

British plan, was ready for the defense of his homeland and his country's capital city.

All of the region is historic ground. Nearby is the site of the ancient Aegospotomas river, where another fateful battle was waged. There, in 405 B.C., Lysander and his Spartans defeated the Athenian Navy in the culminating battle of the Peloponnesian Wars.

Assuming command of what he believed to be the single most important spot to stop the British Navy was a heavy responsibility for Mustafa Kemal.

"In fact, to assume such responsibility was no simple affair; but because I decided not to live after the ruin of my country, I accepted the responsibility with all due pride," he said.

Before dawn on the morning of August 10, 1915, Colonel Mustafa Kemal raced his slender, badly supplied forces against overwhelming odds to the ridges where he knew the main thrust of the enemy would be made—to the peaks of Tekke Tepe.

The Turks reached Tekke Tepe first. Once again he won his race against time and both outguessed and outmaneuvered the British commanders, with their superior weapons and fresh and well-outfitted troops.

"I had come to the conclusion," Mustafa said later in writing of the battle that day, "that we could defeat the enemy by means of a sudden, surprise assault.

"To achieve this we needed more than numbers," he added. "We needed a cool and courageous command."

In those precious predawn hours, Colonel Mustafa

Kemal personally led a silent bayonet charge. His men, with fixed bayonets, and his officers, with drawn swords, poured into the enemy entrenchments.

"It was a kind of hell," he would later report of the hand-to-hand combat.

"Our troops stood to it, and maintained, by many a deed of daring, the old traditions of their race."

Mustafa was bursting with pride at the valorous conduct of his battle-weary troops.

Later, Mustafa Kemal would attribute this victory, against such really incredible odds, to the basic strength of the Turkish soldier and the element of surprise in the attack.

"The great monument is Mehmedjik [the Turkish equivalent of G.I. Joe], himself," he remarked many years later when revisiting the battlefield where he had earned the title "Hero of the Dardanelles."

The official British historian of the battle would write otherwise. "Seldom in history," he reported, "can the exertions of a single divisional commander have exercised so profound an influence not only on the battle, but perhaps on the fate of the campaign and even on the destiny of a nation."

6

Disaster in Araby

The struggle for control of the Dardanelles, known in Turkey as Canakkale Boagzi, was over. The Turks had won the battle. The Allies withdrew, never to undertake the invasion plan again.

For England the price of trying to force a way through the Straits was high—205,000 casualties. The French lost 47,000 men.

British poet Rupert Brooke, who died on the Gallipoli battlefield, left these stirring words behind him as a monument to the British efforts to force a path to Constantinople:

If I should die, think only this of me:
That there's some corner of a foreign field
That is forever England.

Though the battle for Gallipoli had been won, the war itself went on.

On the Russian front far to the East, toward the Caucasus Mountain frontier that Turkey shares with the U.S.S.R. even today, the struggle had reached a horrifying ruthlessness.

Unspeakable cruelties and terrifying wantonness spread in eastern Turkey, where a virtual civil war had begun between the diverse elements of the Empire's populations.

Enver had, in fact, persuaded the Sultan that the success of Turkey's (and Germany's) war aims were dependent on the loyalty of his subjects, who could be controlled through their religious beliefs.

As Caliph of the Mohammedan world, the Sultan had then issued a *jihad* (a holy proclamation) calling on Moslems everywhere to stand together for Islam in the war.

As a result, a "holy" war erupted and was kept in motion as Turkish policy in the eastern provinces of the Anatolian mainland. Tens of thousands of innocent Christians, including women and children, were massacred by fanatic Turkish Moslems.

Although instigated by the Turkish government, this underground war was carried out largely by the Moslem Kurds of the region against their Christian Assyrian and Armenian neighbors.

The policy backfired. Kurdish tribesmen remained

loyal, but their Christian neighbors in the region did not.

In fact, in many cases whole villages deserted and aided the advancing Russian army along the entire frontier.

It was to this hopelessly confused front that the newly promoted General Mustafa Kemal was sent.

His fame as the "Hero of the Dardanelles" preceded him. In spite of the chaotic, dispirited conditions he found and the fact that supplies were running short and medicine was almost nonexistent, Mustafa was able to inspire his men, imbued as they were with the legends of his invincibility, to renewed efforts to hold their ground against the advancing Russian armies.

Here again, his quick understanding of the battlefield situation and his rapid decisions were important in helping him to regroup the forces at hand and regain some of the lost territory on this hopeless front. Despite the fact that his forces were below par, they succeeded in pushing the Russians back and recaptured the Turkish cities of Van, Bitlis and Mus, lost in the first Russian advance.

General Kemal also attempted to push an offensive to take the more distant Russian port city of Batum on the Black Sea. He was unsuccessful in this attempt. In midwinter, Russia again gained the initiative and pushed the Turkish forces back to the Russo-Turkish frontier.

One of the darkest pages in Turkish history was written during that cruel, cold winter. A mass deportation of the Armenian people was ordered by the government. This mass exodus, which has become known as the Armenian massacres, was ruthlessly imposed. Over two million people were involved, and it has been estimated that some six hundred thousand lost their lives because of the primitiveness of the methods of transportation, and the camp internment centers to which these people, whom the Turks judged as disloyal, were sent.

Evidence of the disloyalty of the Armenians does exist in the official records of the large numbers who deserted from the Turkish Army and then volunteered in the Russian Army. Then, too, the official Armenian Orthodox Church had issued a proclamation early in the war urging all Armenians to give support to his Most Christian Majesty, the Russian Czar Nicholas.

The ugly bestiality of the deportations, however, is an infamous page on Turkey's ledger and generated a most intense hatred for the Turks among all remaining Armenians.

A meeting here on this wild, cold front with Colonel Izmet, the new Army Chief of Staff on the Russian front, was important to Kemal's future. The two would form an alliance and close friendship in their mutual distaste for the policies and programs of Enver's Committee Government.

Their personal conversations and dreams for Turkey's future would later blossom into sound programs to rebuild the country. Izmet, capable and experienced in administrative work, would be an important ally in the Turkish War of Liberation which followed World War I.

On this same frontier, Kemal would also meet another reliable and capable officer—Kiazim Kara Bekir. Bekir, a big, heavyset, industrious and rigidly honest man, was serving as second in command to Izmet, and he too would one day play a major role as Kemal became Turkey's Man of the Hour.

But the work of war went on.

The Russian front, already known as the Front of the Dead, was a bitter experience for these three patriotic men. Fortunately for all three, the Russian Revolution was already threatening, and the strategic importance of the area was lessened when Russia withdrew from the war.

General Kemal was next sent to Syria. Here an urgent task faced the Turks on a broad, ill-defined front. A major debacle threatened them in Arabia.

At the beginning of the war, the Empire embraced most of the Arabian peninsula except Aden and the states of the Persian Gulf. But, as Kemal knew from his earlier service in exile in Syria, much of the area was actually not under control of Turkish authorities, and the loyalty of its people was suspect.

Then, too, the proclamation of the Caliph-Sultan's *jihad,* signed by all the highest religious leaders in the

Empire, did not produce the solidarity of purpose in Enver's dream of a pan-Islamic federation—even in the Arabic world of the Empire.

The Arab tribesmen defected and revolted in large numbers despite the awesomeness of the decree of their spiritual leader, "the shadow of god on earth." As a result, the British gained valuable allies in these subject peoples in their campaign throughout Arabia.

Even in western Arabia, the Sultan failed to hold the loyalty of the important Arabian chieftain Prince Hussein, who declared war on Turkey and joined the British forces of General Sir Edmund Lord Allenby and one of his chief architects of Arabian policy in the Middle East, Colonel T. E. Lawrence. Lawrence, the already legendary and knowledgeable Lawrence of Arabia, was instrumental in propelling the Arab Nationalist movement, called the Arab Revolt, into the British camp. And Lawrence's vast desert army, led by Hussein's son, Faisal, was of enormous aid in pushing the Turks back.

The ingeniously well-conceived guerrilla war tactics of the British, the superior quality of their equipment and forces and the passionately nationalistic Arab movement had already created one catastrophe after another for the Turks before Kemal arrived. They were being pushed slowly but steadily across the entire Arabian Peninsula.

Kemal was, in fact, first sent into Syria to carry out an evacuation of the Turkish forces there. The plan was abandoned.

Instead, he was ordered to report as a Corps Commander to the Seventh Army under German General von Falkenheim, in a hastily conceived offensive. Von Falkenheim's plan—the forming of a lightning army group—was aimed at the recapture of Bagdad, deep in the Syrian desert in what is today Iraq.

The project, known by the code name Yilderim ("lightning"), was an ill-advised and ambitious undertaking. The Germans sent in an entire German brigade as reinforcement for the Turkish forces for the operation.

Kemal, who knew the Arab world and its terrain well, argued unsuccessfully against the plan. He objected to the enormity of the project and the lack of really top forces to undertake it.

In a report to the High Command, he stressed the need of a better-equipped force merely to hold what they still retained in Syria. He explained, too, that the Turkish Army was ill fed, ill clothed and too demoralized for an offensive action against the British forces which held Bagdad.

"The opinion I reached then was the same which I expressed at the first moment of entering the Great War . . . that the German Army and the group dependent on it would be defeated," he said with pessimism.

When his advice went unheeded, Kemal sadly resigned his command and left the front to confer with the War Minister in Constantinople.

Kemal had been right. The von Falkenheim plan was finally abandoned as the British overran all of Palestine (much of present-day Israel and Jordan), and von Falkenheim was relieved of his command.

Mustafa Kemal was immediately called back to the Syrian front to take command of the Seventh Army there, now again under the over-all command of his former superior, General Liman von Sanders, with whom he had served on the Gallipoli front.

Kemal trusted and admired Liman Pasha, in contrast to his dim view of most of the German high command. Realizing that much of the Empire was irretrievably lost —already Mecca, Bagdad and Jerusalem, three of the holiest cities of the Moslem world, were in enemy hands —the two searched for a realistic strategy.

They formulated a plan to hold an east-west line across the top of Palestine, from near Jaffa on the coast (modern-day Tel Aviv) to the strategic Hedjaz Railway.

The position commanded the route to Damascus. Mustafa Kemal's Seventh Army was to hold the center of the line. With him were his old friends General Ali Fuad and Colonel Izmet, who had been on his staff on the Russian front. The Fourth Army was to cover the railroad, and the Eighth and Twenty-Second the line to the sea.

Conditions were almost hopeless. Lawrence of Arabia described it brilliantly. He told of the plight of the almost unmechanized Turkish Army, reporting that the hungry Turks "were destroying their own power of movement by eating their transport [horses and mules], which they could no longer feed."

The British-Arab forces had an over-all superiority of

two to one and an overwhelming advantage in both cavalry and air support. Interestingly, in this arid part of the world above the Dead Sea, British fighter planes were bombing the Turks from an altitude of six hundred feet below sea level.

The Turkish forces in that hostile land fought them off with rifles, often the only weapons they had, from twelve hundred feet below sea level.

Morale was at an all-time low.

"The population hates our government and looks forward to the arrival of the British," Kemal gloomily wrote to a friend. "And the enemy is strong in men and transport, while we are like a thread of cotton before them."

The best he could do, as the commander of the Turkish force, was to attempt an orderly retreat.

Kemal set his sights on retreat to Damascus. But arriving there, he saw that defense was useless.

Already the brilliant, even spectacular exploits of Lawrence and Hussein's son, Faisal, had cut him off. The advance of those forces and the British under Allenby had led to anti-Turkish uprisings from hitherto loyal Syrian and Transjordan tribes and caused many desertions among the Arabs still in the Ottoman Army.

On October 1, 1918, the British and Arab forces entered Damascus, and the remainder of Syria fell.

The British air power had converted the retreat into a rout, and the destruction of telephone and telegraph lines had even cut the Turks off from communication with Constantinople.

Kemal, exceeding his orders as he had done at Gallipoli, withdrew the remnants of his forces of the Seventh and Fourth armies beyond Aleppo, on the extreme northern border of Syria.

Here he intended to bar the enemy's entrance into Turkey proper. And the line of evacuation and withdrawal he planned—and held—in those rugged mountains corresponds approximately to what is modern Turkey's southern border.

Mustafa Kemal indeed knew the terrain and his people well.

His decision to withdraw the disillusioned and scattered Turkish forces, who were still harassed by Allenby and Lawrence's Arabs, to what he considered a defensible frontier would mean that the Turks would be defending their true homeland.

Once again, Kemal won his race against time. His weary troops, some of whom had been on the move on the battlefield for more than six months without respite, were given a chance to rest before having to defend the area.

"And this time we shall be defending Turkish soil," he said fiercely.

Kemal knew his Turks would fight well.

"My country is at stake," he said of his actions in defending them before a German commanding officer, who promised reinforcements which never came.

To his old companion General Ali Fuad, he confided that there actually was a compensation for the retreat and loss of Syria. "It will be in the establishment of a new, better-defined state, consisting of the Anatolian lands north of Syria, peopled by Turks.

"Ben olacegin" ("I am a Turk") he muttered with pride.

The end was not far off. All Rumeli (Turkey in Europe save Gallipoli) and a small section of land adjoining Constantinople was gone.

The battle in which the Turks defended a line from Antakya on the Mediterranean Coast to the north of Aleppo (present-day Halep in Syria) can be considered the last battle between the Ottoman armies and the British-Arab forces in World War I—and the first in the Turkish War of Independence.

It was here on Turkish soil that Mustafa Kemal formulated many of his emerging ideas about the national struggle that was soon to come.

A few days later, on October 30, 1918, the Armistice was signed at Mondros, ending the hostilities in this theater of World War I.

Under the terms of the Armistice, the Germans were to leave Turkey. Mustafa Kemal took over the complete command of the demilitarized front.

7

Aftermath of War

The Armistice did not end the hostilities.

It was true that the Turkish Army no longer faced annihilation. But in Kemal's eyes, the dismemberment of the Turkish state by the victorious Allies was a worse fate.

When the Treaty of Mondros was signed aboard the British battleship *H.M.S. Agamemnon,* lying at anchor off the coast of the Island of Lemnos in late October, 1918, no safeguards had been agreed upon regarding the integrity of the Turkish homeland. Nor had any agreement been reached as to the ultimate solution of what the Allies called "the Eastern Question on Turkey."

Documents showing secret accords between the Allied partners did reveal that Imperial Russia had been promised Constantinople and the western coast of the

Bosporus, the Dardanelles and the Sea of Marmara—which, of coruse, would give her a long-sought outlet to warm seas. (The agreement was not fulfilled, however, when Russia withdrew from the war and the Russian Revolution toppled the Imperial government).

Arabia, according to the secret agreements, was to become an independent state; Italy was to have a share of the Mediterranean coast of Antalya; France would have Syria; and England would get Bagdad and the ports of Haifa and Acre.

There were other agreements between the Allies of the Entente, often contradicting one another. All had one thing in common—the dismemberment of the Ottoman Empire.

Kemal, who realized that the Allies fully intended to divide the Empire, felt that all was not lost. He thought that the Turkish state of Anatolia could be preserved, and he was determined to stop partition there.

"Morally and materially, the enemy powers were openly attacking the Ottoman Empire and the country itself," he said. "They were determined to disintegrate and annihilate both."

An informal agreement had been reached with the British delegate aboard the *Agamemnon* that the Greeks would not be allowed to occupy Smyrna (Izmir) and that no occupational troops would be landed in Constantinople.

"But the allied powers did not think it necessary to observe the provisions of this agreement," Kemal said.

73

And he was right. On February 8, 1919, French troops entered Constantinople and placed it under international control. It was the first spark to flame the fire of rebellion against the disorganized Ottoman government now led by Izzet Pashet, who had replaced the rule of the Committee government under Enver. Enver, Talaat and several other of the Young Turks had in fact fled to Germany on the day of the Armistice, leaving the Ottoman Empire in ruins.

"The Sultan-Caliph had one sole anxiety—namely, to save his own life and comfort," Kemal said with contempt of the new government. "And many members of the government had the same feeling, so without being aware of it the nation no longer had anyone to lead it, but lived in darkness and uncertainty, waiting to see what would happen next."

The bitter pill of occupation of the capital was taken with sullen sadness as the troops entered the city led by an officer riding a huge white stallion—an ironic gift from the Greek population of Constantinople. It was reminiscent to the Turks of the days long ago, when the conquerer Sultan Mehmet had taken the city five hundred years before and consolidated Moslem rule on the shores of Europe.

He, too, had ridden gloriously through the fallen Byzantium city upon a white horse as he paraded through the streets of the then mostly Christian city.

"Those who began to understand clearly the terrors

and extent of the catastrophe began then to seek some means to save the country," Kemal told friends.

"In seeking ways to save the situation, it was considered especially important to avoid irritating the great powers—England, France and Italy," he added.

"But again, the main point was that the Turkish nation should live in honor and dignity."

But how?

A final, agonizing blow came when an agreement was reached by the victorious allies at the Peace Conference in Paris. It fell like a thunderbolt on the defeated Turks.

The Greeks were granted their formal claim to take possession of the port of Smyrna, on the Anatolian mainland coast of the Aegean Sea.

The resulting occupation of the beautiful, palm-fringed harbor city, coupled with a massacre of part of the Turkish population, spurred the many still fragmented Turkish patriotic groups into action.

What was needed was a national leader.

And that leader was to be Mustafa Kemal Pasha!

"Events will provide a commander," he had once said to a junior officer in the darkest hours of Gallipoli. And they had.

Now they did so again.

"The nation that exerts every imaginable effort and makes every possible sacrifice to rescue its freedom and independence cannot help being successful," he declared to those who doubted the wisdom of action against the allies.

His most powerful arguments were reiterated—that the Turkish nation must live free if honor and dignity were to survive.

"And such a condition can only be attained by complete independence," he declared passionately.

"For no matter how wealthy or prosperous a nation is, if it is deprived of its independence it no longer deserves to be regarded otherwise than as a slave in the eyes of the civilized world," he warned those who counseled caution.

As Kemal saw the Ottoman Empire everywhere in ruins and dismembered, it seemed a time for action.

Only the fatherland, affording protection to a mere handful of Turks, remains," he pointed out. "And it is now suggested also to divide this.

"In these circumstances, one resolution alone was possible. And that was to form a New Turkish state— the sovereignty and independence of which would be unreservedly recognized," he said later.

However, he needed a pretext to leave Constantinople and learn more of the mood of the country in order to organize a rebellion of the people against the puppet government of the Sultan and Izzet Pasha, his Grand Vizier.

Fortunately, the Allies unwittingly aided him in his plan.

Disorders and riots had spread in the interior as Turkish bands fought minority Greek, Kurd and Armenian countrymen. Clearly someone was needed to quell the growing disorders and put an end to the killings—someone whom the people trusted and admired.

Kemal, with his wartime record and the esteem in which he was held throughout Turkey, was a natural choice of his government. With the approval of the Allies, he was sent into the interior of the country.

He was named Inspector General of the Turkish Anatolian lands, between the waters of the Black Sea on the north and the Mediterranean on the south. The post gave him command of all Turkish troops with instructions to combine the military and civil authorities. His broad orders, prepared with the aid of friends high in government circles who were in sympathy with Kemal's secret plans for organizing rebellion, gave him the right to issue instructions to all the governors in the provinces of the Anatolian interior.

"I felt as if a cage had been opened, and as if I were a bird ready to open my wings and fly through the sky," he said with exhilaration about his new post.

He immediately set to work organizing his staff officers—all men known personally to him and devoted to the liberal principles he himself espoused. They were a cadre of hand-picked men who could aid him in establishing the organization of the Turkish Army in a rebellion that would drive the French, the Italians and, most especially, the Greeks from Turkish soil.

"This was the resolution we adopted before we left

Istanbul and which we planned to put into execution immediately after we set foot on Anadolu [Anatolia] soil at Samsun," he said.

Nine days after Kemal landed at Samsun, an important Black Sea port that almost exactly divides the Turkish Anatolian mainland in two, he asked all military commanders and all civil authorities to promote vigorous national demonstrations in favor of Turkish independence. This was hardly what the Ottoman Sultanate or the Allies' Occupational Government had in mind when they sent him into Anatolia to act to quell the disorders there.

His letter to the Governors was indeed curious. Kemal had sent it only to those authorities whom he considered safe.

tional independence are in danger," he wrote. He suggested that a truly national body be set up to legally carry out the responsibilities to preserve Turkish rights.

When the Ministry of War learned of his action, they "The territorial integrity of the fatherland and our naattempted to recall him immediately. But it was too late. Again the victorious Allies played into Kemal's hand as the Greek Army marched inland from Smyrna and bands of Greek irregulars attacked the Turks at Samsun.

These actions enabled Kemal to swiftly rouse thousands of discontented Anatolian Turks, who were willing to fight to hold back the Greek Armies.

Mustafa Kemal then sent out orders in the Sultan's name ordering all army commanders to cease surrendering arms to the allied invaders—clearly an open and flagrant violation of the peace treaty the Sultan had signed at Mondros.

A typical answer was the reply of one patriotic corps commander: "In case of any attempt at occupation by the enemy, the Twenty-Third Division will not surrender its position, and if it is attacked it will defend it, recruiting reinforcements from among the inhabitants."

It was exactly the reply Kemal expected.

He again proved that he knew his Turkish countrymen well.

He got in touch with two of Turkey's most influential generals, both serving as commanders of Turkish forces in Anatolia. They were his old friends Kiazim Kara Bekir and Ali Fuad, with whom he had served on both the Syrian and the Russian fronts during the Great War.

He patiently explained to both of them that there was hope for Turkish independence if they would reassemble their armies and fight by his side.

Persuading them was no easy task, for both men, high-ranking officers in the Ottoman Government Army, while sharing his views on the tragedy of Turkey's position, were loyal to the Sultan. Both, however, were passionately devoted to the need for Turkish freedom.

"For such a nation as ours, destruction is better than living as a slave," Kemal argued, explaining that they were compelled by events to rebel against the Ottoman Government.

"We have to bring the whole nation and the army into a state of rebellion," he said.

"For with a pretext for each action, the Allied fleets

79

and soldiers were in Constantinople; the provinces of Adana were occupied by the French; at Antalya and Konya were the Italian military.

"On every side there are foreign officers, officials and private people, plotting to dismember Turkey," he explained with a desperate urgency.

"Therefore, Independence or Death."

Those words were to become the battle cry to free Turkey as Kemal, with at first only a handful of adherents, slashed out and with a titanic will forged a modern state.

Kemal was convinced that the terrible danger of national extinction was upon Turkey. Immediately after gaining Kiazim Kara Bekir's and Ali Fuad's support, he sent in his resignation as Inspector General of the Anatolian provinces. He also resigned his commission as a general in the Ottoman Army.

And so, as has happened time and time again in history, the long war after the war began.

Bringing the Turkish forces up to strength necessary to fight on the broad fronts threatening the country was no easy task. Arms and ammunition were needed.

As for men, Kemal knew he could rely on his Turks.

The Turkish soldiers who had laid down their arms as a defeated army following the Armistice were somewhat apathetic at first about being recalled to a cause that seemed hopeless, but the landing of the Greek Army at Smyrna and their advance inland was too much to bear. The march of the Greeks and the wanton pillage and burning of Turkish villages that resulted was a decisive factor in sparking Turkish courage and determination.

Kemal was, of course, certain of success. "The possibility of failure cannot be dreamed of in the case of a nation that is full of life and capable of making every sacrifice," he said.

He did indeed know his Turks when the nation was at stake. And he immediately put into effect an elaborate arms procurement plan. Raids on Allied ammunition supply dumps by men loyal to his cause were executed with great daring and bravery. If caught, these men were summarily shot as traitors to the Ottoman regime. And the risks were great. Both Allied and Ottoman troops were on the lookout for the rebels everywhere.

By the third week in June, Kemal had already summoned a Congress of Civil Delegates to meet at the small city of Sivas, deep within the Anatolian mainland, to take up the matter of Turkish independence.

"Independence or Death," Kemal declared, while insisting that the rebel delegates conform with the spirit and form of democracy and legality.

In early July he called a preliminary conference which was set up at Erzurum, far to the east, where a few individuals could work out the practical problems to be discussed to legalize the rebellion as a national movement.

When the rebel delegates met briefly at Erzurum, they gave Mustafa Kemal the recognition he felt would be required by electing him their chairman. The preliminary conference held there set up a permanent organization, the Action Committee for the Defense of National Rights, that ultimately actually functioned as an arm of government of Turkey.

Here at Erzurum, far in Asian Turkey in the vast brooding Anatolian mountains which are covered by a permanent mantle of snow, the delegates, with Kemal at their head, set forth the principles of the War of Liberation the rebels would wage for their country's freedom.

Erzurum was a fitting choice. Old before man had a written history, the site has known the prehistoric Hurri, the Uratu, the Assyrian, the Commerian and the Sythian conquerers. Xerxes conquered the city in the fourth century B.C., and it knew Alexander, Anthony and Tamerlane.

The city is completely surrounded on all sides by majestic mountains, dominated by the conical Mount Ararat, where Noah was believed to have landed the Ark after the flood in Biblical times. Her other great mountains, Ala Dag and Dumler Dag, give birth to the Euphrates river, whose magical waters flow through Mesopotamia's legendary fertile crescent and have fathered the birth of civilization itself. Nearby Master Dag, another snow covered mountain, provides the source of the mighty Tigris river.

The city itself is a natural fortress, six thousand feet above sea level, with a harsh climate of Arctic-like winters and seeringly hot summers. The terrain and climate are matched by the hardy endurance of the people of the area.

It was here the delegates met in a simple schoolhouse on the 23rd of July, 1919, and set about the business of nation building.

Kemal, as Chairman, addressed them with patriotic fervor.

"I emphasized the fact to them that it was surely impossible to imagine that there was one patriot in the country who was not already aware of the dark and tragic dangers that surrounded us, and who was not deeply stirred by them," he said later in discussing those historic moments.

"History will never fail to recognize the existence and the rights of a nation," he said, urging the delegates to action and raising their spirits for the cause he knew they faced.

Kemal was sure that rebellion was the only route to save Turkey and supremely confident that he was the man to lead the nation.

"Whose existence is it essential to save? And with whose help? And how?" he asked.

"In these circumstances," he pleaded, "one resolution is possible—namely, to create a New Turkish state, the sovereignty and independence of which would be unreservedly recognized."

The main principles and conclusions for independence were laid here—the city where the War of Liberation for Turkey was born. The delegates officially stated that resistance would be offered to *any* occupation of Turkish soil. They also set the date for the broader, more truly national assembly that would meet in Sivas in September to decide the country's political future.

Kemal dominated the Erzurum Conference and forced an acceptance of the idea that the Turkish homeland did not embrace the Arab world as the Ottoman Empire had. This was a novel idea to many of the more conservative delegates, but Kemal had learned in the bitter defeat in Syria the tragic lesson of a Turkey dying from overstrain in an attempt to hold on to Empire.

"It was an unwilling empire," he said in persuading the delegates of the folly of attempting to recoup it.

Kemal had learned another lesson, too. The Allies were just as sick of war as were the Turks.

He talked of what he suspected—that many in the West no longer really cared what actually happened to Turkey and hardly felt themselves responsible to push the Greek cause to annex Turkish territory.

In setting up a legal apparatus, the Action Committee for the Defense of National Rights, Kemal shrewdly guessed that the Turks might get recognition of their rights to exist although a defeated country, if they insisted only on the integrity of the Turkish homeland.

When questioned by the American Government Commission sent to Turkey from the Peace Conference to assess the aims of the Nationalist Movement, Kemal could openly explain the need for self-preservation of exclusively Turkish soil.

"I had a long conversation with General Harboard of the American Commission," Kemal explained later, "on the question of the aims of the National Movement, its organization and the main factors that would contribute to the establishment of national unity."

"I only mention the matter, incidentally, to tell you that he respected my reply," he added with the knowledge that the movement he founded already had a moral and legal basis because of the manner in which it was set up at Erzurum.

8

The Rebels Plan Resistance

The congress which convened in Sivas in September drew delegates from all parts of the country—some even secretly from Rumeli (Turkey in Europe)—and set up a small permanent body of representatives who would become the Acting Government for Turkey throughout the War of Liberation.

Mustafa Kemal, who was named President of the Congress, saw to it that all acts and principles passed by the delegates were drawn up with correct parliamentary procedures.

He saw to it, too, that the delegates spelled out that the major aim of the rebel nationalistic movement was solely to preserve the territorial integrity of Turkey. The document drawn up would be known as the National Pact.

"The country is one whole, and no parts of it can or shall be detached from it," it declared.

The delegates also further affirmed that they were the legal government of Turkey and that, since the capital was under occupation and the government of the Sultan was subject to foreign control and incapable of governing the Turks, the new national government must be independent of Constantinople.

These were bold actions.

Kemal was jubilant, for these were words and actions all of the delegates, even the most conservative of their constituents in the provinces across the length and breadth of the fatherland, could endorse enthusiastically.

"It was essential that the entire nation take up arms against whoever would venture to attack the fatherland of the Turks and Turkish independence," he said.

"It would undoubtedly have been of little advantage if we had made clear to the public at the very beginning all the implications of our resolutions which were of such far-reaching importance . . . and . . . it was necessary to proceed by stages, utilizing all opportunities to prepare the feeling and the spirit of the nation and to reach our aim by degrees."

As a national struggle, carried on for the sole purpose of delivering the country from foreign invasion, Kemal's plan worked—for all its boldness in a tradition-ruled society such as the Ottoman Empire had been.

No less bold was the arrogant telegram Kemal sent to

Constantinople, breaking off relations with the Ottoman Government.

"You are nothing but cowards and criminals; you cabal with our enemies to betray the nation," he said.

"But do not forget that the nation will remember your irresponsibilities, when she comes to pronounce sentence on the infamies that you are committing," he warned in his wire to the Sultan's Cabinet.

The new government Kemal envisioned, even in these early days, was to be one no Eastern nation had ever known—that of strict parliamentary procedure and democracy—limited as it was. There would be no more autocratic rule by the Sultan-Caliph, with his hold on his subjects that permitted no independent thought. And there would be no more military rule, such as the Enver Committee Government had been.

"Government will be a groundswell of thought from among the people arising from the heart of the nation itself," he said confidently.

Kemal also sought to ensure that the Allies would not be dealing with a mere puppet regime but, instead, with a broadly based national force with positive aims and programs, conscious of its rights and struggling to rise phoenixlike "from the ashes of the Ottoman Empire."

The National Pact was a declaration not only against the craven, puppet government of the Sultan but also against the Allies' plans to dismember the fatherland of the Turks.

Kemal then issued a proclamation from Sivas, as the actual *de facto* government of Turkey, calling for national elections—with the elected deputies enpowered to select the form of executive government desired.

After summarily severing relations with Constantinople, Kemal cut all telegraph and telephone lines to the capital and issued orders to have all official government correspondence directed to him in what would be the new Turkish capital—Angora (modern-day Ankara).

He again chose his capital well, remembering the sophistication and decay of Constantinople from his military school days.

Angora in the fall of 1919 was a mere town; but it was situated in the heartland of Anatolia, and it was perhaps more typically Turkish than most larger centers—certainly more Turkish than Constantinople, with its cosmopolitan and foreign influences. It lies on a central plateau, three thousand feet above sea level, among the pale beige and brownish rolling uplands from which the mountains of the highlands rise in steep and craggy precipices. The old town, established before the written history of man, as was Erzurum, was the ancient capital of the Hittites.

Angora's old citadel, even today, has winding, crooked streets or alleys that rise ever upward, spilling into small cobblestone courtyards and the homes of its very, very poor inhabitants.

In 1919 all that existed was the ancient citadel, a railroad station—part of the German-built Bagdad Railroad line—the School of Agriculture, situated on the outskirts of the town, and a few dilapidated buildings.

It was no city at all. But to Kemal it represented a part of the unquenchable Turkish spirit and a fresh start for a new nation in the making. It was here that he established the provisional government of the nation. His government building was a rude schoolhouse.

Frightened at Kemalist strength, the Sultan's government thought to counter the nationalist rebel movement by reorganizing itself and forming a new cabinet.

One of the members was sent to Angora to confer with Mustafa Kemal. Together they agreed that further Turkish integrity would be strictly adhered to and that no privileges would be accorded to either minorities or foreigners in any part of the country. All would observe Turkish rule and respect her sovereignty.

It was further agreed between the Sultan's delegate and Kemal that new national elections would be held and a Congress convened, although the Sultan's minister insisted that the Congress meet in the true capital of the country—Constantinople.

The fly in the ointment, as Mustafa Kemal saw it, was this provision. He desired that the delegates to the new Congress meet in Angora, where Nationalist strength lay, but he was overruled by fellow Nationalists in his provisional government.

Kemal, who was a duly elected delegate from Erzurum, decided after some thought not to go to the Sultan's Congressional convention. He warned many of his fellow Nationalist deputies not to attend either.

"Constantinople, being under foreign occupation, was not a very favorable spot for the deputies to carry out their legislative duties unmolested," he said, as he protested against the meeting place.

But most of the deputies, even some most loyal to Kemal, felt they had nothing to fear. Besides, many felt that now that they no longer held the stigma of being rebels and outlaws and were legally elected deputies and legislators of government, the Sultan's umbrella of government was safe.

So, as the new year 1920 dawned, the majority went to Constantinople for the opening session of the Sultan's parliament.

It was to prove a mistake, as Kemal had warned.

As the deputies assembled, the Allies again played into Kemal's hands.

In an incredibly ill-timed decision, the occupational government decided on a full-scale occupation of the capital. This was not a mere show of force—as had been the earlier case, when Allied troops entered the city in small but well-paraded numbers—but occupation by a major military and civil government force. The decision was made to occupy all government buildings—the post office, the telegraph office, every important edifice—and these buildings were forcibly taken by British soldiers and sailors.

At the same time, a halfhearted attempt was made by the Allies to re-establish the Independence of Armenia, a minority state within the boundaries of the Turkish homeland.

Earlier, at the Treaty of Sèvres, the Allies had, in fact, recognized a sovereign Armenia which the Armenians in Turkey had proclaimed at the close of World War I. But they had not actively supported the "paper" state, and, of course, the Nationalist rebel provisional government of Kemal never recognized it.

The result was more outbreaks of violence in the Armenian-Turkish areas.

Then, as if this was not enough, the Allied Forces, with the complicity of the Sultan, occupied the Assembly building and arrested and deported as many Nationalist delegates as they could get their hands on.

The move was made, apparently, on the mistaken assumption that it would put an end to the Kemalist National movement of rebellion.

How mistaken the Sultan and the Allied Governors were.

"Our military intelligence had never been more thoroughly unintelligent," Lloyd George, Britain's chief negotiator at the Paris Peace Conference, admitted.

Mustafa Kemal's earlier warning and predictions that the delegates not go to Constantinople, which he considered "unsafe," again served to boost his stock among those deputies who escaped arrest and added to his legend as a leader among the soldiers and the peasantry.

Now Kemal was in a position to call a new assembly in Angora and denounce the Sultan as a traitor to Turkish independence.

"All these events," he said of the formal occupation of the capital and the arrest of the Turkish delegates to the assembly called in Constantinople, "have made it necessary to call together an Extraordinary Assembly which shall have the administration of the State and the Nation under their control and in their authority."

Kemal then telegraphed a protest to the various representatives of the Allied Powers in Constantinople and the Foreign Ministers of all neutral countries.

"The blows struck have reduced the rightful political sovereignty and freedom of the Turkish nation," he said.

His telegrams pointed out the "sacredness of the struggle" of the Nationalist movement, which had been organized for the rightful preservation of Turkish independence.

"No power could deprive a nation of the right to live," he declared passionately.

His pleas affected many in Paris.

One European diplomat branded the terms levied against Turkey as "the most punitive of peace arrangements and one of the most daring and deliberate divisions of the spoils of war in modern history."

The newly convened assembly delegation represented a

new breed of Turk. Many had reached Angora while being hunted down by Allied soldiers or fellow Turks in the Ottoman Army of the Sultan.

And they were once more branded rebels and traitors! A *fetva*, a legal proclamation of the Sultan-Caliph, had been issued and distributed throughout the country against them. The *fetva* asked, in typical Islamic fashion, the following rhetorical question: "Is it permissible to kill these rebels?"

And, again in typical Islamic language, the proclaimed reply was: "Yes, It is your duty [as Moslems] to do so."

But still the deputies came to Mustafa Kemal's Angora headquarters.

There was nation building to be done and a new war to be waged to rid Turkey of the invaders pouring into the country.

On Friday, April 23, 1920, the members of the first Turkish Grand National Assembly, with Mustafa Kemal at their head, passed solemnly through the ranks of soldiers who lined the dusty streets of Angora, to begin a new era for Turkey.

The day would mark the beginning of a Turkey whose face would henceforth be turned westward. It sounded, too, the first peals of the death knell of the Ottoman regime.

9

The War of Independence

Despite the need to forge a new political atmosphere and spur his supporters on in the dream of carving a new Turkish State from the ruins of Empire and the debacle of a lost war, Mustafa Kemal had a second serious task at hand.

The foreign invaders must be driven from the land.

The badly equipped army, however, needed ammunition and guns. Fortunately, the underground supply routes which Kemal had set up earlier when he had first arrived at Samsun as the Sultan's Inspector General were functioning well.

Most of the stolen armaments were shipped to the little port of Inebolu, on the Black Sea almost directly north of Angora. The port had two natural outcrops of rock with a narrow channel between, forming a natural year-round harbor which gave the dockside some shelter and respite from the fierce winter winds blowing across the Black Sea.

From Inebolu the smuggled armaments were carried overland to Angora.

This was a prodigious task. Even cannons, some secretly procured in the occupied capital of Constantinople under the watchful eyes of Allied guards, were dismantled and sent overland.

The supply route was maintained through the efforts of a human chain of dedicated patriots—men, women and children—who carried the stolen goods on their backs over the rugged Anatolian uplands and across the wild mountains. In winter the rutted roads were sometimes impassable. Deep snow drifts barred passage to the few motor vehicles available.

Winston Churchill, later writing of the incredible efforts of the Turks against the tremendous odds, said that Kemal "called upon the wives and daughters of his soldiers to do the work of the camels and oxen which he lacked."

To add to the hardships, further civil strife had to be dealt with. Already uprisings between the anti-Nationalist forces of the Sultan and Kemal's Nationalist guerrilla bands were flaring up across the land.

"The flaming fire of rebellion raged," Kemal said of the tragic warfare amongst the Turks.

He knew they should be united and fighting the real enemy—the foreign invaders—instead of each other.

"A nation that asserts and maintains its unity and its will sooner or later will be able to bring any proud enemy who attacks it to suffer," he said.

"For this reason it is surely more important to suppress the upheavals in the country," he added in support of his arguments to fellow Nationalists on why his small army was dealing first with the uprisings fomented by those loyal to the Sultan rather than with the Greek Army in the region of Smyrna.

Trying to keep the Assembly deputies under control was to continue to be a difficult and tedious task; but it was a political necessity.

Kemal exercised great patience in this political homework.

"The only practical and safe road to success lay in dealing with each problem at the right time. This was the way to ensure development and restoration of the nation," he explained.

Besides, it was still necessary to do much work to ready the Turkish Army for the conflict which lay ahead to push the Greeks into the sea.

In reorganizing the Turkish forces, Kemal brought Izmet to Angora to serve as his Chief of Staff. He also called on his longtime political and military friend Ali Fuad and a man named Refet to serve under Izmet.

Refet, who had been living among the guerrilla forces in the area near Smyrna under the pseudonym Aydin Efe, would prove a daring and dashing commander in the field and of invaluable help. Ali Fuad would prove adept in helping Kemal with some of the myriad political problems he faced and in working with the Assembly.

But it would be Izmet, with his careful, cautious administrative talents, whom Kemal could turn to best. Izmet, an able soldier, would also carve himself a glorious reputation in battle.

The Nationalist Assembly, with careful prodding by Kemal and Ali Fuad, at this time concluded a treaty with the Revolutionary Russian Soviet government through which Turkey would receive much-needed supplies and ammunition. It would be of inestimable help in outfitting the army.

And again, by chance, the Allies played a major role in deciding the fate of the Nationalists—and the future of Mustafa Kemal—in signing the Treaty of Sèvres with the Sultan. The treaty, with its harsh provisions, officially carved up all of Turkey for the Allies.

"The Treaty of Sèvres is for the Turkish nation . . . a sinister sentence of death," Kemal said with anguish at its savage terms.

"We cannot enter into dealings based on trust with nations that do not banish from their minds this treaty. From our point of view it does not exist," he added.

In the words of Winston Churchill, the treaty was "like fresh fuel thrown on a smoldering fire of hatred."

Even conservative American statesman Charles Evans Hughes, who was then serving as Secretary of State, showed great misgivings about the terms imposed on

Turkey. He wrote that they "were severer than those of the European peace treaties and not only depriving the Turks of vast territories but imposing upon them even greater measures of foreign control than they had had before the war."

Most agonizing of all for the Turks were the provisions that gave Smyrna, European Thrace (Turkish Rumeli) and almost a score of Turkish islands in the Aegean Sea to the Greeks.

The treaty terms, for all their savagery, were provident for Kemal. The balance now tipped completely in favor of the Nationalist cause and united the entire nation behind him in full support of his crusade to fight for Turkish independence.

Already King Constantine of Greece had landed on the Anatolian Coast to personally conduct the war in the Greek land grab of Turkish soil. Constantine, interestingly, landed at the site where Richard the Lion-Hearted came to reclaim the Holy Lands during the Crusades. Constantine was the first Christian monarch to set foot on Turkish soil since the Middle Ages.

At first the Greek armies, supplied by England with superior weapons, claimed victory after victory. They quickly overran the Turkish forces, taking the holy Moslem city of Brusa and then Eskisher in the deep heartland of Asiatic Anatolia.

"To Angora," was the Greek battle cry.

Soon the sounds and rumblings of cannon and the twing of bursting shrapnel could be heard in the Assembly hall in Kemal's capital.

"Whatever happens, we're going to remain in this country," he told his followers, even when defeat seemed so near.

"We're going to defend every hill," he added. "We're going to die under our flag."

In these dark hours when defeat stared at them, the Nationalist Assembly prepared to move eastward to Sivas, situated on a fortresslike plateau deep in the interior of Anatolia.

To guard against possible treachery at home, the Nationalists then set up a series of emergency military tribunals which could, if necessary, summon, condemn and execute "traitors" to the cause of independence.

Although legally set up and responsible to the Nationalist Assembly, the tribunals were designed to help Kemal act speedily—and ruthlessly—to curb dissent. They were called Independence Tribunals, but would later earn a somewhat odious reputation as instruments of death for Kemal's political enemies.

Kemal, his political front protected, finally readied his army to move against the advancing Greeks. He decided to form his front lines on the shores of the Sakarya, one of the three great rivers of Anatolia.

It was here, on a sixty-two-mile front under blazing, white-hot August heat, that the Turks prepared to take a stand.

The stuttering of machine-gun fire, the roar of artillery and the shell fire made the earth shake. Vast tides of Moslem Turks tore into the Greek Army in an effort to protect their homeland.

King Constantine must have had visions of an empire in Asia, as had Alexander the Great so many centuries before. His armies poured onto the hot Anatolian plateau of this historical land. The site of the battle was near the city of Gordian, where Alexander had trod before and had cut the Gordian Knot prior to forging an Asian empire for the Greeks. The thought that perhaps now the Greeks could again hold sway in this ancient land must certainly have occurred to the Greek monarch.

But Mustafa Kemal thought otherwise.

He had prepared his army well. "We shall drive the Greeks before us as chaff in an Anatolian gale," he said confidently as he directed the Turkish lines to hold firm.

He personally rode patrol duty along the front while directing a battery of field telephones to keep in touch with his commanders. Sleeping only in short catnaps, he was everywhere, extolling his Turks to hold the line.

His strategy was to blow up rail and communication lines to the coast and Constantinople and then attack supply caravans on the Greeks' already overextended supply lines.

Though the Greek Army had superior weapons and surplus planes supplied them by the French and British, who had used the aircraft so successfully against the Turks in Syria in World War I, Kemal reported that

101

Greek casualties in the first nine days of battle were twice what the Turk casualties were.

The Greeks were fighting, of course, on a hostile, alien land, while the Turks were fighting on terrain they knew well. It was Turkish homeland, and the Turks fought well; but the Greek advance held. After seventeen days of fierce battle, much of it hand-to-hand combat with bayonets, they were able to hammer the Turks back.

The Greeks finally crossed the Sakarya river and moved eastward toward Angora. Here the warfare became an especially brutal and tragic war of reprisal and savage vengeance. Hideous bloodbaths between the two armies occurred, with no quarter given or taken on either side.

The battleground was atop mounds of ancient Phrygians, including the grave site of the legendary King Gordius himself.

Here the Turkish Army dug in.

Finally, the Greeks began to fall back—their supplies of food and water running short as the battle raged on those parched and blazing hot uplands and hills through which miles and miles of trenches had been dug.

Kemal's strategy was paying off for the Turks.

"Death" was Kemal's order to his Turks.

When the Greeks retreated, the exhausted Turks could not follow, and an informal cease-fire was arranged. During the long months of stalemate that developed, both armies reorganized. Fortunately for the still less well-prepared Turks, a secret peace pact was concluded with the French on the Syrian border.

The peace pact freed 80,000 Turkish soldiers for the coming offensive, in which Kemal planned to drive the Greek Army completely out of Anatolia.

During the cease-fire, Kemal was given the nation's highest honor, the title Ghazi, meaning "the Victorious" or "Conqueror" and "Destroyer of Christians." He was also named Commander-in-Chief of the Army and Dictator of Turkey by the National Assembly.

At the same time, he had to face another grave political crisis—a peace movement begun by his political enemies, who wanted to come to terms with both the Greeks and the British on any terms.

To this the Ghazi would not agree.

"Turkey for the Turks" was the Kemalist motto.

Acting alone, as Dictator of the country, Kemal personally signed the death warrants for twenty-five Turkish officers—many of whom had been his former comrades-in-arms. They were charged with treason against the state and were executed by the Independence Tribunals he had set up.

There would be much criticism of his action; but, as Dictator, Kemal effectively silenced this opposition.

By the following summer, Kemal's Turks were ready to begin the massive offensive he had so carefully planned to drive the Greeks out of Turkey.

He dreamed, too, of a second offensive to force the British out of occupied Constantinople.

"Those damnable foreigners will get out of Turkish lands and waters or we'll blow them out," he boasted to his staff officers.

The long winter had sapped the enemy's strength and morale, for much of Anatolia is stark and forbidding. It is as harshly cold and windy in the winter as it is harshly hot in summer. But to the Turks, whose homeland it is, it proved a tonic. Morale was high throughout the army.

Now the front was again west of Sakarya at Dumlupinar and Afyan. Beyond lay Smyrna—the prize.

When his army was ready, Kemal struck. At midnight on August 26, 1922, a carefully organized offensive was launched.

With an intense bombardment, conducted by the Turks with a surprisingly large cache of stolen or captured enemy weapons, Kemal's army hit the Greek lines. And they crumbled, as Kemal had predicted, "like chaff before a gale."

The Ghazi personally led the major attack and had the satisfaction of seeing the Greek Army flee in disorder, abandoning their supplies, their weapons and even, in many cases, their transport.

"Turks," he shouted. "Go forward, your goal is the sea."

By the end of August, there was virtually little of the Greek Army left. Its remnants rushed to Smyrna to waiting Allied ships in the burning harbor—but not before an awful toll in human lives, including civilian women and children, was taken. The savagery only drove the Turks on faster to exterminate the Greeks.

Finally, on September 9, 1922, the victorious Mustafa Kemal rode triumphantly into Smyrna in a gala motor-cade. His victory was marred by his vengeful Turkish troops, who began a reign of terror in the already blood-drenched city.

Smyrna was taken but the war itself went on, and the brutality of the murdering and looting among the Greek and foreign civilian population of the city would tarnish the Ghazi's reputation abroad.

Now that the Greeks had been thrown out of Anatolia, they began a campaign to march upon Constantinople from the former Turkish Rumeli territory they held in Europe.

To counteract this move, Kemal's Turks marched from the shores at Smyrna along the sea to strike at the Greek Army.

One Turkish Army entered Canakkale, near the site of ancient Troy, but was stopped there by an Allied Army of Occupation under the British general Sir Charles Harington.

Here a direct confrontation, not with the hated Greeks but with a major Allied power, took place. Each side cautiously waited and wondered who would fire first.

The situation was ominous, without question, for it could have led to a new war between the still ill-prepared Nationalist forces of Turkey and the British—the greatest naval power in the world at that time.

Each side held its position—and waited.

Fortunately and dramatically, it was announced to the watching, waiting armies that a new armistice had been signed. The Treaty of Mundanya, signed October 11, 1922, was a complete turnabout for the Allies and a victory for the Kemalists.

In it, the Allies agreed to the return of Eastern Thrace and Andrianople to the Turks. The Nationalist representative at the peace table, Izmet, agreed to Allied terms for continuing international control of the straits of the Bosporus.

With the reins of government now firmly in Nationalist hands, Mustafa Kemal could work at his dream of national unity for the Turks—and the creation of a modern state. The Sultan's government in Constantinople had ceased to have any authority in the country.

"Friends," he would say to the people of Angora on his triumphant entry into the city, "this victory in Anatolia will remain the finest example in history of how powerful and how lifegiving a force belongs to an idea fully adopted by a nation."

"After destroying and overcoming one by one the obstacles that rose before us, we shall achieve at last all that is necessary for us to live happy, prosperous and free."

10

Nation Building

The treaty of Mundanya truly began a new era for Turkey. In the treaty settlement, the Turks regained European Thrace (Rumeli), and the demilitarized straits were returned upon the agreement that they would be open to all nations in time of peace and to all nations in time of war if Turkey remained a neutral nation.

Although Mustafa Kemal had already been given the sole power of Dictatorship and Commander-in-Chief of the Armed Forces during the War of Independence, he was now elected President of the National Assembly.

At last the real work of nation building could begin according to the ideas and views of its chief architect, the Ghazi, Mustafa Kemal. Strife in the land between foreigner and Turk was over. So, too, was strife and bloodshed between brother Turks to become a thing of the past.

"We want nothing else but to live free and independent within our national frontiers," the Ghazi told the deputies of the National Assembly in Angora. "And the Turkish people and the Turkish Grand National Assembly and its government defiantly persist in their demand for the recognition of their right to existence, freedom and independence, like every civilized nation and government. This is our cause."

In setting forth his first peacetime programs for Turkey, Kemal reminded his listeners that much still remained to be done in the land.

"After this struggle, that has lasted three and a half years, from the scientific point of view and from the economic point of view, we shall continue our fight, and I am sure that we will be successful," he said.

Already Kemal had clearly outlined his ideas for reforms to take place in education before a conference of teachers and representatives of the University of Constantinople. He pointed out the importance of the school in the lives of the children of Turkey.

"Our most important and greatest duty is to be successful, whatever happens, in the matter of education," he said.

But a matter of vital political concern—who should be the delegates to the new peace treaty to be set up by the Allies at Lausanne—was also of paramount importance if Turkey was indeed to live free and independent and pursue its own destiny as a nation. The new peace terms, as the Ghazi saw them, would abrogate the detested Treaty of Sêvres (signed in 1920), which gave the victorious Allies the right to dismember Asiatic Turkey.

Again Kemal selected his able and efficient administrator, Izmet, to lead the Turkish delegation at the peace table. The National Assembly carried out his wishes, and appointed Izmet the country's Foreign Minister and the chief negotiator at the peace conference.

Resistance from the isolated Sultan's cabinet in Constantinople was instantaneous. The Sultan and his Grand Vizier wished to lead the peace delegation at Lausanne. But the National Assembly refused them recognition and a statement signed by 80 members of the Assembly, including Mustafa Kemal, declared by decree that the Ottoman Empire was extinct.

They proclaimed, too, that a new Turkish state had been created and that the Turkish Constitution ordained that the right of sovereignty belonged not to the Sultan-Caliph but to the nation.

"Sovereignty belongs unconditionally to the nation . . . and is based on the principle of the active and personal administration of its destiny by the people."

The deputies reiterated the fact that the Assembly had never recognized the legality of the government of the Sultan, who had opposed the national liberation.

The Sultan's continued interference in the affairs that rightly belonged to the National Assembly government

109

in Angora and the indignation of the deputies over the actions of the Sultan played into the Ghazi's already planned move.

The Sultanate must be abolished!

"Sovereignty and the sultanate are not given to any person by discussion," he argued before the Assembly. "Sovereignty and sultanate are taken by strength, force and violence.

"The sons of Osman [the first Ottoman leader] seized the sovereignty and the sultanate of the Turkish nation by violence," he said. "This usurpation has lasted for six centuries. And now the Turkish nation, warning these aggressors of the end of their power, has revolted and actually taken into its hands sovereignty. . . . This is an accomplished fact." Kemal's conviction reflected his desire to secure the deputies' vote for an immediate separation of the Sultanate and Caliphate and the overthrow of the Sultan.

The Ghazi, whose real intent it was to abolish both the Sultanate and the religious Caliphate domination over Turkey, was well aware that the time was not yet ripe to dispose of the Caliphate. But by separating the two, he could subtly pursue a divide-and-conquer posture that would eventually mean the end of both.

"Some heads will roll," he warned his listeners, should the accomplished fact of the peaceful and legal transfer of sovereignty to the Assembly from the Sultanate not be accomplished.

His persuasive argument and his warnings to those

standing in his way were heeded. The deputies passed the needed legislation to dissolve the government in Constantinople, and the orderly transfer of the reins of government was officially accomplished on November 4, 1922. By November 5, the Turkish delegation to the peace table in Lausanne, under the leadership of Izmet, set out for Angora.

Shortly thereafter, it was learned that the Sultan had secretly left Constantinople in a British warship, the *Malaya*. He was immediately exiled from Turkish soil and deposed from the Caliphate by the National Assembly.

A member of the Ottoman dynasty was then named Caliph. His role, however, was to be strictly religious.

"Away with the dreams and shadows—I have banished the Sultan and the rottenness of the Ottoman Empire," Mustafa Kemal is reported to have said following his victory.

He spoke, too, of the need to control the power of the new Caliph as a strictly religious leader.

"Sovereignty does not admit any sharing in any meaning or form, any shade or kind," he added with nationalistic fervor that won his listeners to his views.

Although foreign affairs were of paramount importance if Turkey's destiny as a nation was to be secure, domestic political rivalries had sprung up in an effort by many Assembly deputies to curb the Ghazi's growing power and strength.

As the time approached for the new national elections to be held, according to the provisions of the Turkish Constitution, opponents of Mustafa Kemal brought forth a bill to be considered by the National Assembly. It would have deprived him of his right to be re-elected to the Assembly—and thus destroy his political base.

The proposed bill stated that a candidate to the Assembly or to public office had to be from the people within the current Turkish frontiers. Of course, Salonika, Kemal's birthplace, was outside the post–World War I frontiers and to this day belongs to Greece. The bill further insisted that all candidates had to have been residents of the area from which they would be elected for at least five years. This provision would serve to deprive Mustafa Kemal and many of his army cohorts of the right to stand for election to the Assembly.

Kemal protested heatedly.

"Unfortunately, the place where I was born lies outside the present frontiers, and I have not been established in any electoral area for five years," he said. "The reason for this is that the enemies who wanted to destroy our whole country and nation have been partially successful. But, if our enemies had been completely successful . . . , even those gentlemen who have signed here might have been born outside the frontiers of the country," he reminded his listeners.

He went on to point out that it was not possible for him or many of the Assembly members who fought in the Great War and the War of Independence that followed to reside in one place for five years because of the service they had been performing for their country and its people.

"If I had been condemned to stay in one place for five years, I could not have carried out my defense at Airburnu and Anafartalar on Gallipoli, which saved Constantinople . . . and I could not have resisted enemy expansion after the capture of Bitlis and Mus.

"If I had wanted to fulfill the conditions laid down by these gentlemen, it would have been necessary for me not to have formed an army at Aleppo from the remains of the armies evacuating Syria and resisted the enemy and actively establishing what today we call our national frontier." His emotional and patriotic appeal won over both his listeners in the Assembly halls in Angora and the people of the nation when they learned of it.

As a result, strong protests at the attempt to deprive the Ghazi of his rights as a citizen were heard throughout Turkey. Mustafa Kemal knew his Turks and their sense of patriotism well.

Astutely, he realized he would have to become a successful politician with a planned program of reform and a broadly based political party behind him to see that voices of reaction in the nation—such as those expressed by his political enemies in the Assembly, many of whom did not want to see reforms in the Turkish system—would not destroy the principles for which the War of Independence had been waged.

He then began a tour of many of the major cities in the nation to organize what he called "the People's Party," based on the principles of Western-style popular government.

Kemal eagerly sought out people in all walks of life to give him their views on the necessary reforms.

In an interview in an Angora newspaper, he pointed out the need to develop a program that would benefit all.

"We must develop as far as possible the aptitudes and abilities of our nation, and make use of all the sources of wealth of the country," he said.

"The People's Party will be a school for the political education of our people," he commented in one of the cities he visited. This won him wide support from the people of a land that had never known popular government, who were earnestly eager to participate in determining the country's future.

During his tour to acquaint the common people with the facts of political awareness, the Treaty of Lausanne was signed. In the treaty, signed July 24, 1923, Izmet had been able to clear up almost all points of difference between Turkey and the Allies, including the abolishment of the hated "capitulations" under which foreign nationals enjoyed a special favored position and did not have to observe Turkish law as did the Turks themselves.

"This treaty," Kemal told his delighted listeners wherever he went, "is a political victory the likes of which was not seen in the entire history of the Ottoman period."

The Treaty of Lausanne represented a remarkable victory for the Turks. To Kemal, with his love of his country and determination to make Turkey a free and respected nation, the victory must have been very sweet indeed.

The Turkish delegation at the conference table, headed by Izmet Pasha, had gone to Lausanne to fight the combined Allied delegations of Great Britain, France, Italy, Rumania, Yugoslavia, Japan, Greece and even the United States (attending as an advisory nation). And they triumphed, securing Turkish territorial integrity, ending the hated capitulations and receiving the recognition of the West, which only a few months before had continued to support the tottering, decaying Sultanate.

Izmet Pasha was the true hero of the hour, for he singlehandedly had hammered home the points of dearest interest to Turkey's future.

"Sovereignty, sovereignty, sovereignty" had been the Turkish tune, and he played it until the Allies gave in on all major Turkish demands.

Even though some of the Allies were still behaving like wolves on a scent, sure that the Nationalists would crumble when they came into contact with the cold light of reality of Western interests, Izmet stood firm. He even went so far as to refuse to sign the first draft of the treaty as presented by the Allies at the first session.

"Izmet Pasha won a great diplomatic victory at Lausanne and stood all the Allied diplomats on their heads," said Joseph C. Grew, chief of the American delegation at the peace conference.

Most Western diplomats admitted that Turkey had an important advantage in having a victorious army behind her as her delegation took their places at the conference table to settle her future. This was quite different, of course, from the period during which the Treaty of Sêvres had been signed by the dying government of a whipped nation following the debacle of World War I.

The question of the hated capitulations was uppermost on the agenda of Kemal's nationalist delegation—and uppermost, too, as far as the Allies were concerned.

Great Britain, in particular, was adamant about the continuation of the favored treatment of foreign nationals.

The Western nations had a legitimate point. While the concessions had granted foreigners a special and privileged status which the Ottoman subjects of the Sultan did not enjoy, they had safeguarded foreigners from often extreme treatment.

For example, Turkish law as set down by the Koran was a primitive one. The "eye for an eye" and "tooth for a tooth" philosophy prevailed in the religion-dominated courts of the Ottoman regime. The result was often cruel and inhuman punishment, even for minor offenses.

Under the capitulations, foreign nationals were not subject to Turkish law or Turkish courts and were tried by their own national laws. Financial concessions were also made to and for foreign businesses and businessmen which were unfair to the Turkish subjects. Foreign nationals were even exempt from paying taxes, whereas the Turks were heavily taxed by the Sultanate.

To the Nationalists, the capitulations were odious— a symbol of the decadence of the nation under the Ottomans. They signified a basic weakness that was humiliating to a sovereign nation.

"Sovereignty, sovereignty," Izmet repeated again and again in his low, almost whisperlike voice.

"The capitulations must go," he would add time and time again in discussions.

He did agree that appropriate guarantees would be made to foreign nationals and patiently explained that the Turkish position was dictated by strong national feelings at home.

He finally won his point, and the French and Italian delegations, not really any longer as concerned with upholding the capitulations, surrendered first.

Lord Curzon, the chief British negotiator at the conference, realized he was being deserted by his allies and finally gave in too.

"All they wanted was out on any terms," he said bitterly at the time in criticism of Britain's Entente war partners.

Izmet also stood firm against the massive economic

grants and reparations at first demanded by the Allies.

The dispute over reparations from the Turko-Greek War precipitated one of the most serious crises at the conference. The conference, in fact, actually hung on the brink of rupture over the matter.

During the last phase of the conference, the Greeks attempted to force settlement in favor of Greece in all eastern Thrace. This was another point to which Izmet and his delegation would not agree. Fortunately, pressures were applied on the Greek government by the Allies and a compromise was reached. The Greeks agreed to back down on their demands, and the Turks, in turn, agreed to make concessions concerning their demands for reparations against the Greeks—but not before the Greek Minister of Foreign Affairs went so far as to declare that Greece would go to war rather than concede.

Their actions might have again plunged these war-weary nations—east and west—into conflagration.

The British, in fact, sent the battleship *The Iron Duke* into the Straits to back up Greek demands. Faced with public opposition at home and a desertion of the Greek stand by the other allies, the British finally backed down on this point also.

Izmet had one trump card, which he played skillfully at the conference table through the long months.

None of the great powers desired or intended to fight —and Izmet knew it. He was also shrewd enough to see that the Allies were disunited, each with its own interests paramount, and was able to win on a divide-and-conquer basis.

Several important questions were not solved at the conference, but were agreed to later by Turkey and each individual nation. One of these questions was the disposition of the oil-rich Mosul district of Turkey, which the British refused to return. The final solution was arrived at in 1926 under an Anglo-Turkish Treaty, in which a portion of the disputed territory was returned to Turkey and she was granted royalties from the oil fields in the section retained by the British.

Cruelest of all the decisions reached was that concerning the resettlement of minority populations in the disputed areas. The agreements were criticized during the conference and afterward as inhuman.

In the population moves, some 1,500,000 Greeks were resettled in Greece with incalculable suffering. The exchange also affected five hundred thousand Turks, who were more easily assimilated in the vast, underpopulated Anatolian areas of Turkey.

Numerous historians of the period noted that the bitterness and bloody reprisals taken between Greeks and Turks after the Greek invasion made any other solution impractical.

The Treaty of Lausanne gave Turkey what Kemal demanded—the end of Allied occupation and the end of the capitulations. It strengthened his hand against his few political rivals at home.

119

11

The Awakening of a Nation

Secure in the strength and popularity of his programs for Turkey, with a new and just peace treaty with the Allies that had broad appeal, the Ghazi prepared to amend the Constitution and proclaim Turkey a republic with an elected president as head of state.

Turkey was ready for nationhood. And Mustafa Kemal, the Ghazi, was her leading citizen.

"I demand that we change the system. And I have decided that Turkey become, here and now, a republic," he declared dictatorially in the Assembly halls on the night of October 29, 1923.

So swiftly did he act and so skillfully did he move that there was no time for what little remained of the opposition to make a countermove. The Kemalist faction was in control.

So, amid cries of "Long live the Republic," the Ghazi's

bill was quickly passed into law by the Assembly. The time was 8:30 P.M.

At 8:45 P.M., Mustafa Kemal was elected the nation's first President and head of state. He would continue to hold his title as President of the Grand National Assembly as well.

"Turkey is a Republic, and I am its first President," he said with glowing pride and obvious satisfaction.

"We shall all go forward together," he told Angora's excited citizens the following day as the establishment of the Republic was being celebrated to the firing of 101 guns.

Simultaneously, the evacuation of Constantinople took place, an event the Ghazi carefully staged. As the Allies marched away amid cheering throngs in the streets of the beautiful city, the Union Jack, the French Tricolor and the American Stars and Stripes were slowly lowered from the official administration buildings and the Turkish flag of crimson red with a white crescent and star was dramatically raised to take its rightful place above the crowded streets.

Amid the jubilance and rejoicing across the land, some dissent was heard. Several newspaper editors in Constantinople criticized what they felt to be the rather high-handed manner in which the Republic had been proclaimed. And, of course, there were still many in the land, particularly in Constantinople, who supported the Caliph and were suspicious of a republican form of government.

So, despite the rejoicing, there was much work for Mustafa Kemal to do. Turkey must join the twentieth century.

To Kemal, this meant doing away with the Caliphate.

"So long as the Caliph exists, there is no possibility of the social and secular reforms which I have in mind," he told friends.

Kemal rightly sensed that many dissatisfied by the declaration of a Republic might use the Caliph to foment problems and erect stumbling blocks on the road to progress.

There were also those, opposing Kemal's reforms who wished to use the Caliph and the Caliphate, with its tight hold on the minds of the religiously dominated people of old Turkey, to further their own political ambitions.

This Kemal would not tolerate. Even before the Treaty of Lausanne had been signed, he had gone throughout Anatolia and insisted in his speeches that the very idea of the Caliphate was a bankrupt one. But he had trod softly then. Now Kemal felt that the time was ripe.

For Turkey, the past would die hard as the people stubbornly clung to the old traditions and the old culture and religion as dictated by Islamic law.

Turkey had been dragged into the twentieth century, but she was in Kemal's eyes and those of most progressives, saddled with a Caliph who still presumably headed all the Moslem states in the world.

Before Turkey could assume her rightful place among the nations of the world, the Caliphate had to be destroyed.

The Caliph, Abdul Mejid, a member of the former Ottoman ruling family, had been duly "elected" by the National Assembly after the abolition of the Sultanate, with limited religious scope. He had, in Mustafa Kemal's view, exceeded his authority and had sought to impose secular opinions as well as religious opinions on his Moslem flock and on Turkey itself.

One deputy in the Assembly had already sought to organize a political party around the person of the Caliph, insisting in his petition that the Caliph was the Assembly and the Assembly "belonged" to the Caliph.

This required an immediate decision.

"The Caliph must go," Kemal vehemently told his friends and political supporters at a meeting he called in Izmir (Smyrna).

A strong argument for abolition of the Caliphate was the obvious fact that as long as the Caliph existed, Turkey itself was tied down to the laws of the Koran— already thirteen centuries old. So outmoded were these religious laws that there would be no possibility of enacting the social and educational reforms so necessary to modernize the nation as long as they were allowed to be observed.

By the end of February, 1924, Kemal, his prime minister, Izmet, and several officers of the army agreed to approach the Assembly and abolish the title completely.

123

On March 1, 1924, in his opening speech before the Grand National Assembly session, Mustafa Kemal pitted his popularity against any and all enemies of reform and eloquently spoke before the deputies.

"Our greatest strength, our prestige in the eyes of the world, depends on the new form and the new character of our regime," he said. "And nobody, whether he is Caliph or by any other title, can participate in the new direction of the destiny of this nation."

Kemal, measuring his audience carefully, quietly said: "We must, therefore, proclaim the deposition of the Caliph . . . , for the New Turkey and the people of the New Turkey have no reason to think of anything but their own existence and their own welfare."

These were strong words, even before the Assembly. Its members were mainly relatively sophisticated and educated men, but they held deeply to former religious training and backgrounds.

Kemal then insisted that a law be passed to end forever Turkey's dependence on past Ottoman codes of conduct and to liberate her new republican government from the stranglehold they had held on the people.

So persuasive and carefully planned was this bold new action that the laws were pushed through immediately. On March 3, 1924, the Caliphate was abolished and all members of the Imperial Ottoman family were forever banished from Turkish soil.

"If the French today, a hundred years after the Revolution, are still of the opinion that it is dangerous to their independence and sovereignty to allow members of the royal family to come to France, we on our part should be eager to see to it that those who see on the horizon the sun of absolute power being allowed to rise again cannot sacrifice our Republic."

Then taking advantage of his audiences' fears of the possibility of some dark forces' overthrowing the Republic for which they had sacrificed so much, Kemal subtly said: "The Republic should now and in the future be perpetually and definitely immune from attacks."

"Our grandfathers in the past have established a high civilization," Kemal added, "but these old civilizations could not be considered adequate for us as a nation in modern life."

Having swept the old religious order out of the country was not enough. Mustafa Kemal was determined to turn Turkish society upside down if necessary to achieve his aims—and much still stood in the way of progress.

His next step was to attack Turkish law—much of which was outmoded and, of course, dictated by Islamic rulings from the Koran.

His fast course of action to change the face of Turkey overnight not only aroused the traditionalists and religious leaders of the country but even alienated some of his friends. Already three of his comrades from the War of Liberation and military school days stood in opposition to Kemal's autocratic methods.

Kiazim Kara Bekir, without whose aid he would not have been able to reform the Turkish Army for the War of Liberation, and Refet, both staunch Republicans and Kemalists, broke with Kemal.

Kiazim Kara Bekir put it succinctly and realistically for all:

"I am in favor of the Republic. But I am against personal rule."

Even Ali Fuad, whom Kemal had known during his student days in Constantinople and with whom he had spent many a languid free afternoon reading poetry, had become estranged. Fuad was for the Republic and he was for social reform and change, but he felt it should proceed gradually in an evolutionary way, step by step, rather than in the revolutionary manner the Ghazi had chosen to pursue.

Despite the growing opposition, even among old and trusted friends and devoted Nationalists, the Ghazi remained determined.

Turkey would join the twentieth century—now—by force, if necessary.

"It is a fact that is not open to doubt," the Ghazi said in a dramatic speech at the time, "that in the Turkish Republic, in place of the old rules of life and of the old law, are new rules of life and new laws."

He immediately organized a committee of experts to prepare a new Turkish Civil Law to replace that which had grown out of the teaching of the Koran, written in the seventh century A.D., which no longer met the requirements of life in a modern state. Under the old law, under which large parts of the Moslem world lived and some do even today, if a person was caught stealing—even so small a thing as a loaf of bread—his arm was cut off. The thinking behind such laws, Kemal felt, was clearly not fitted to a modern nation such as he was determined Turkey would be.

Kemal had already seen that modification or reform of the old law was not enough.

"For the needs of the Turkish nation a new code of civil law is necessary," he said as he directed his panel of twenty-six experts from the Ministry of Justice to study the matter.

The result was a code of law based on the newest, most practical and most democratic code of civil law in the world—that of the Swiss.

After fourteen months of work, a Turkish Civil Law was readied for a vote in the National Assembly. With his usual persuasive ability, coupled with a few threats, the Ghazi assured passage of the new code.

"An important achievement has been made in the legal sphere of our struggle for independence by the acceptance of the Turkish Civil Law Code," he would say later.

And, of course, the Ghazi was correct. With the passage of the new code, the shackles of centuries were burst open and the nation passed from a civilization ruled by a religious edict, or *fetva* (which was, in effect, a legal but religious command), to a contemporary civilization in step with the fresh winds blowing across the East from the West.

In foreign affairs, the new Turkish Civil Code put an end to accusations by Western European states that Christians living in Turkey had to defend their rights before Islamic courts which had, of course, been hostile to them—or, at least, more likely to side with a Moslem.

The new code set in motion vast changes. For one, it was instantly recognized that the Constitution would have to be revised and become as secular as the Turkish law. The new provisions deleted the clause that the Turkish state was Islam.

So all-embracing were the changes that Mustafa Kemal was finally able to destroy the hold of the hojas and other sects, such as the dervishes, that had always controlled education in the state.

The Ghazi went so far as to banish the costume traditionally worn by the religious leaders—the turban and long gown. On a tour of the countryside after passage of his law banning the garb of religious persons, Kemal spotted a turbaned hoja in a crowd in a small city in the province of Ushak. So seriously did he regard the infraction of the new law that he ordered the Governor of the province be imprisoned and the town leveled. However, when the order was submitted to him next day, the Ghazi shamefacedly canceled it. But he had certainly made his point.

Destroying the power of the hojas was no easy task. It struck at the heart of the mores and traditions the people of Turkey had followed for centuries. Unlike the

Caliph, who was a remote, though all-powerful figure and the shadow of God on earth and who lived in the equally remote Dolma Bache Palace in Constantinople, the hoja held a firm and real grasp on every village.

It was the hoja who educated the children of Turkey. It was the hoja who interpreted the Koran and civil proclamations of government and read the news to the mainly illiterate Turkish peasants. And it was the hoja who actually regulated the daily life of the Turk. For the religion of Islam entered into the daily life of individual men, women and children to an astonishing degree. Islam dictated all phases of life, from the way the corner butcher killed a sheep or goat to where and how prayer was said each day.

The stranglehold of the hoja and Islamic law was real, and Kemal, once he had abolished the religious courts and set up a Civil Code of Law for Turkey outside the Islamic religion, knew he had to challenge the viselike grip of the hoja and religious elders on Turkey's educational system if he was to succeed.

He directed that all educational institutions of the Republic be placed under the secular Directorate of the Ministry of Public Education. The result was an emancipation of school children and students from the strict edicts of the Koran, as interpreted by a hoja, in favor of a Europeanized general education.

Kemal had long felt that the system of the religious schools could not meet the requirements of a modern

129

society. In the hoja schools, apart from instruction in religion and morals, only a minimal education in writing and basic arithmetic was attempted.

Even as early as the Sakarya campaign against the Greeks during the War of Independence, the Ghazi had nurtured an ambition to free the Turkish school child.

"I am of the opinion that the methods of education and instruction followed up to now have been the most important agent in the historical decline of our nation," he had said then.

"I intend a culture suitable to our national and historical qualities, remote from the ideas of an age of superstition," he added.

When asked what he intended to do once the war had been won, he had replied: "My greatest ambition is to try to raise the standard of national enlightenment."

It had been a momentous year—and not only for Turkey.

Mustafa Kemal, at forty-two, married a pretty, petite, brown-haired, brown-eyed young girl he had met in Smyrna.

She had already wholeheartedly embraced the twentieth century. Unlike most Turkish women of her day, she wore no veil. She dressed instead in chic and expensive Parisian gowns.

She was well educated and conversant with the ways of Europe, where she had been sent by her indulgent and wealthy parents for her education.

Her name was Latife.

Latife joined Kemal's household at Chankaya, in the suburbs of Angora. The household already included Kemal's aging mother, Zubeyde, who religiously observed the old ways, never appeared before a male guest in the house without a veil and usually preferred to sit cross-legged on the floor on cushions in the Oriental manner rather than on modern, Western chairs.

The two must have presented a remarkable contrast— not unlike the contrasts in Turkey itself. For Kemal's young bride, who was a thoroughly Westernized hostess, readily joined Kemal's friends and political associates. She was of great help with foreign diplomats and their wives as well, for she could converse fluently with her husband's guests in English, French, Italian and Greek, as well as her native tongue.

Despite Kemal's pride in his talented wife, the marriage —which was childless—ended in failure. And Kemal, while vigorously pushing reform along more progressive Western ideals, resorted to the old Turkish Oriental law and divorced Latife by decree. It was the last such divorce granted in Kemal's modern Turkey.

Kemal's temperament and singleness of purpose in pushing reforms for Turkey—his only love—required great solitude. And with Latife gone and the later death of his mother, he saw less and less of political and diplomatic guests and more of a small coterie of drinking and card-playing companions in his evenings of diversion.

Many, including the devoted Izmet, were shocked by Kemal's surrender to almost nightly drinking bouts and fretted over the toll they took on his health. None, however, could dissuade him from his new habits, nor could one see any visible effect on his performance of his state duties.

12

Turkey in Transition

"For everything in the world, for things material and things moral, for life, for success, the truest guide is knowledge," Kemal told the Assembly deputies as he pushed ahead for reform in education of Turkish youth.

"For it is education which either makes a nation to live free and independent . . . or leaves it a nation of slavery and poverty."

His aims for a compulsory national education program for all Turks would become a peaceful but forceful program as Kemal strove to pull his country out of its backwardness to join the ranks of the nations of the West.

"Our great cause is the raising of our position as the most civilized and most prosperous nation," he said as he admonished opponents of change.

And by civilization, Kemal meant Western ideas of civilization and the complete secularization of Turkish education.

"Leave this nation alone," he warned the traditionalists who still dared voice opposition. "Let the children be educated."

With the Caliphate abolished and the role of the hoja reduced, Kemal could now revamp Turkey's antiquated educational system.

And he set about the task with great vigor, despite the fact that a great part of the nation was a generation trained in religious schools, where even the Turkish language as an academic language was not permitted. Many were not in favor of national education for everyone.

Kemal had to take these things into account as he revised educational standards. Many of his people, nurtured for centuries on thoughts of the next world only, were psychologically unprepared for his progressive programs.

Interestingly, one of the secrets of Kemal's success in turning Turkish education on its ear in the revolutionary programs he instituted was the corps of young teachers and educators who joined his crusade and spread the Kemalist doctrine. They became a dedicated and devoted cadre, and were well compensated for their efforts by a grateful and knowing government.

But reaching the young under a compulsory educational system was not enough.

Trade schools had to be expanded for more practical

schooling. Kemal even opened evening schools for adults.

There had been some contemporary schools in Turkey for many years, such as the secular school Kemal had attended in Salonika, but they had been very few in number. Some, particularly in the cities and larger towns, had been able to benefit from general education, but the peasants had been completely neglected.

"The master of this country and the basic element of our society is the peasant," Kemal declared in a speech explaining his basic policy of national education for everyone.

"And it is the peasant that up to today has remained deprived. Therefore, the educational policy we shall follow is the removal of this pre-existent ignorance."

Since Kemal was the State, his countrymen dutifully trooped to the schoolrooms set up in every hamlet.

So insistent was Kemal, and so capable in enforcing his views on even a reluctant citizenry because of his prestige and viselike grip on the Grand National Assembly which made the laws, that he was finally able to introduce coeducational classes into the entire school program.

This was a very revolutionary step indeed in a society that had heretofore frowned upon allowing adult women and even young girls to mix in society.

To Kemal, educational reform was essential if Turkey was to take her rightful place in the world. But he

135

needed to carry his battle outside the schoolroom and broaden it and direct it to the people. He realized that he would have to be cautious and use discretion in casting away old traditions and remaking Turkish society, but he was determined that he would, by force if necessary, change the life of every Turk—man, woman and child.

He started by arguing persuasively against the dress of his countrymen, striking first against the national male headgear—the fez.

"We are going to adopt the modern, civilized, international mode of dress . . . , including a headdress with a brim," he told one audience, which stood in mute astonishment in Kastamonu, a major city in north central Anatolia.

"The name of the headgear is 'hat,'" he added before the disbelieving eyes of his listeners, who gaped at the hat he held in his hand as he delivered his first famous hat speech.

The speech was a particularly radical, even heretical one, for the fez was the very symbol of Islamic manhood. The wearing of the fez was intimately associated with the daily life and religious habits of the average Turk. It had taken the place of the turban in Turkish society over a century before but, like the turban, was traditionally brimless. According to Islamic law, a man's head needed to be covered at all times, but nothing on the headdress should prevent the wearer's forehead from touching the ground during prayer.

A brimmed hat, therefore, was anathema to the religious practices of the nation. People who wore brimmed hats were called *shapkali,* a derisive term applied to infidels.

As he spoke, Mustafa Kemal bravely waved his brimmed Panama hat before the horrified villagers and appeared bareheaded—another unheard-of revolutionary gesture in a society that had been ruled by strict form.

Mustafa Kemal struck out at other forms of Turkish dress at the same time.

"Civilized international dress is worthy of our nation," he said.

"On our feet shoes; above that, trousers, waistcoat and shirt, tie and jacket; and the natural complement of these, on our heads, peaked or brimmed headgear," he added as he dramatically placed his wide-brimmed Panama hat on his head for all to see.

It was reported that many of the simple villagers immediately raised their eyes skyward to Allah in dread, for fear that the blasphemer, their beloved Ghazi, would be struck dead on the spot.

"You should wear it," Mustafa Kemal calmly told his audience as he showed off his new headgear.

He also argued against the traditional baggy trousers of the Turkish peasant, over which a loose, flowing robe was generally worn.

The Ghazi pointed out that from the material of every Turkish costume two far less costly suits of the Western, international type could be made.

Later, after the National Assembly had passed a law banning the old baggy trousers, robe and fez, Kemal would use more persuasive methods to force his countrymen to change their ancient ways.

The Ghazi actually instructed the local police around the nation to take scissors and cut the seat out of the trousers of men who reverted to the old costume.

A young student would write of the shock in Kastamonu among the villagers, who had been prepared for the Ghazi's visit as that of the coming of a great conqueror—perhaps even on a white horse with sword drawn, as they envisioned the early Ottoman heroes, and certainly sporting a traditional handlebar mustache!

"When the President walked slowly down the street, greeting crowds, there was not a sound. The cleanshaven Ghazi [was] wearing a white, European-style suit, a sports shirt open at the neck and a Panama hat. . . . Only a flutter of hand clapping was all they could muster."

The Turkish hero and conqueror, clean-shaven and fezless, was wearing the dress of the infidel himself!

After attacking the traditional mode of dress merely by advocating that the men change, the Ghazi took a further radical step. He had a law introduced in the National Assembly banning the wearing of both the turban and the fez. (The law is still in effect, and no one in modern Turkey is allowed to wear such headgear. The only place the visitor will see a genuine wine-red fez with black silk tassle is in the antique sections of the Bazaar in Istanbul or, if he is privileged to visit a Turkish home, perhaps in a glassed case or an attic box.)

As an experiment before discarding the fez, Mustafa Kemal had small peaked brims placed on the headgear of the Army. These, he explained, were mainly for reasons of health and to keep the sun from the wearer's eyes.

After his speech before the horrified listeners in Kastamonu, Kemal took bolder steps and advocated that all officials in the realm wear hats. Most of the deputies complied with his request, as did many of the better-educated professional Turks.

Interestingly, the headgear that gained greatest popularity after the banning of the fez was the cap. Even today most of the working-class Turkish men wear drab, gray peaked caps indoors as well as out as a general rule, for after centuries the fez dies hard.

One distinguished writer on Turkey, Lord Kinross, was led to question just why Mustafa Kemal advocated that particular and unbecoming headgear, perpetuating a proletarian Western fashion which was quite transitory and which still retains the aura of "the odd depression look of a Welsh coal miner."

Changing the dress of his fellow Turks was momentous, for in the West, there is and was one recognized mode of dress that distinguished all Westerners. In the

139

Eastern countries, on the other hand, apart from the elaborate Moslem ceremonial, official and religious costumes, there never was a general mode of dress. Religion and climatic conditions usually dictated the costume worn. For women, of course, the veil was mandatory—even for quite young girls in the higher economic brackets.

The Ghazi then took the boldest step of all—emancipation of the women of Turkey. Here he would have to tread even more softly, for it was one thing to clap a brimmed hat on a man and quite another to tear away the veil that traditionally hid the faces of the women.

In one gently worded speech, Kemal pleaded for the women of Turkey, whose position had changed almost not at all since the days of the Prophet Mohammed. "Let them show their faces to the world," he said.

Everywhere he went on his frequent tours within Anatolia, Mustafa Kemal referred to the problem the women of Turkey faced and stressed the importance of the place of women in society, in the family and in their work for the country.

"The reason for the lack of success of our social organization," he explained patiently to one and all, "is from the neglect and defective attitude we have to women."

"If a social organization is content to meet contemporary requirements with only one of the two sexes," he added, "that social organization loses more than half its strength."

During the War of Liberation, Turkish women had played important and sometimes vital roles. Some even bore arms at the front against the enemy. Since women had played such a decisive part in the liberation of the country, Mustafa Kemal felt that they should be allowed to enjoy the fruits of the land they had helped to save.

"One of the necessities of today is to ensure the rise of our women in every way," he told many of his audiences in preparing them for the bold actions he had planned.

In his personal life, Kemal had already began to put into practice what he believed regarding the role of women in the country.

At the time of his marriage to Latife, he had departed from the antiquated Turkish marriage customs. Although it was the rule of the land to have the marriage rites performed without the bride's being present, Kemal had insisted that Latife be included in the ceremony.

After their marriage, he had seen to it that Latife accompanied him on most of his tours of the country. The journeys of the Chief of State and his wife, in a country where it was not customary for a husband and wife ever to travel together, had made a profound impression on the people. Besides, Latife wore no veil and always dressed in Western-style clothes.

Kemal went so far as to organize balls to which Turk-

141

ish men and women were invited. He felt that women should be free to enjoy recreational activities with male citizens as well as work alongside them.

This innovation tore another gaping hole in the very fabric of Turkish society, for even within the sanctity of the Turkish home, women rarely, if ever, joined the men other than in a very formal and inferior position— and always heavily veiled. Only within the female quarters of a typical Turkish home would a woman go about unveiled.

"Our women, like us, are intelligent human beings," Kemal declared in establishing the right of women to join the once almost exclusive male Turkish society.

The Ghazi presided over the first public ball, which he staged in worldly Izmir (Smyrna). Even in this port city, with its relatively sophisticated ways, the ball created quite a stir. The Ghazi impishly invited only Moslem gentlemen and their ladies to the novel party, at which an orchestra played exclusively European dance music.

The Ghazi opened the ball by dancing a fast fox trot wtih the Governor's pretty daughter and then, with frowning glances, let the rest of the gathering know that they were expected to dance together.

Never before had a Turkish woman, no matter how sophisticated, danced with a Turkish man in her own country in public!

Recalling his success in changing the headgear and basic

costume of Turkish men, Kemal turned to the subject of the dress of the Turkish woman.

This was heretical ground indeed, but the Ghazi cleverly appealed to the pride of the Turks, playing upon their emotions as free men in a free society.

"During my journeys, not only in the villages but in the towns and cities too, I have seen our women with thick veils over their faces and eyes," he began in a speech at Inebolu, on the Black Sea.

"Men," he added—"this is the result of our selfishness.

"Let their eyes look on the world. It is necessary. . . . So let us make the sacrifice."

Kemal chose the patriotic port of Inebolu carefully for this appeal, for it had been the men *and women* of that region who had worked so tirelessly to bring the quantities of supplies and armaments stolen from the Allied supply dumps to aid the cause of liberation.

Now he was appealing to them to liberate their women.

But as dictator of his country—yet beloved by the people, who held him in such awe and respect for his accomplishments for the nation—Kemal added a customary word of warning to those who might oppose the new society he was creating.

"No indulgence will be shown to any who try to sabotage this movement of reform," he said. "This is your patriotic duty."

The result was that many women, particularly the younger, better-educated women, threw off their veils and began to mingle in Turkish society. Who could complain at such "patriotic" actions?

Kemal did not cease there. He insisted on complete civil liberties for Turkish women. In 1926, the Grand National Assembly complied with his wishes and passed a bill to that effect.

By 1930 Kemal, who continued to agitate for women's rights, gained them their political rights, too. With the passage of the Municipalities Law, women in Turkey were allowed to stand for public office in city councils. By 1934 Kemal was able to secure passage of legislation that granted women the right to run for any elective office in the land and to participate on equal footing with men in administrative offices of government.

This was a giant step in an Eastern country, for within less than ten years it brought the Turkish woman out of hiding behind her veil and out of the feudal world in which she had previously lived.

Turkish law reforms also abolished plural marriages, uprooting the harem as a way of life.

Kemal had secured for the women of Turkey not only their political and social rights but also their rights as women in the family circle.

He had indeed brought his country a long way in fitting itself into contemporary society.

In almost no other areas of accomplishment was Kemal more proud of success than in having secured educational reforms for Turkey's children and raised the

Turkish woman to a dignified and rightful place in the family.

"Our mothers make us men," he said simply, his eyes clearly on the future of the mothers and men to come.

13 .

The Great Language Reform

The Ghazi was an impatient man. He insisted that Turkey cast off still more of the traditional shackles of the feudal period under which she still labored.

Not to move forward was to stagnate.

One area which needed reform was Turkey's archaic system of dating. Both the Islamic calendar, which begins with the Prophet Mohammed's departure from Mecca in A.D. 622, and the system of telling time in the Islamic world—which begins at sundown rather than at midnight, as in the West—were out of tune with the Western world. To further complicate matters, the Turkish official calendar was based on the Julian year, which had been introduced to the world under Julius Caesar. (The Western world had long since abandoned the Julian calendar in favor of the Gregorian system of days and months which Pope Gregory III devised in 1552.) However, while the Julian calendar was used within the country, foreign correspondence was generally dated according to the universally accepted Gregorian calendar.

The confused triple calendar systems in use led to at least several amusing dating incidents. Tombstones often recorded an Islamic birth date with a Gregorian death date, such as: "Born 1116 [1900], Died 1926."

Kemal's impatience with the inefficiency of his world led him to admonish his countrymen for their stubborn clinging to the old ways and finally to introduce another radical law.

On January 2, 1926, he had the Assembly pass a law which swept away custom and enforced compulsory use of the Gregorian calendar and the use of Greenwich time.

"The year will begin on January 1. The time will begin at 12:00 midnight."

The Ghazi's real objective in pushing through this law was actually the even more far-reaching reform of the Turkish language and its alphabet.

While religious belief, by law, had become a matter of individual conscience and was no longer imposed on a man by the state, Islam still ruled the heart and soul of the average Turk. One special tie remained which Mustafa Kemal was determined to sever—the use of the beautiful but archaic Arabic script in which the Turkish language was still written.

It was the same script that he had detested as a boy in the hoja schools of Salonika.

The artistic characters used in Persia and throughout the Arabic world had been adopted primarily for religious reasons. Arabic was the script of Islam, and since the time when the Turks had accepted Islam as the religion of the Empire, Arabic and Arabic script had been elevated as a language superior to the Turkish in use by the people as a whole.

The characters were complex, numerous and difficult to execute without careful training, and the spellings were erratic.

The Bible in the West had long been printed in the vernacular, national languages, but by decree of the Caliph it was still forbidden to translate the religious books of Islam into Turkish.

The knowledge of Arabic, as a result, came to be regarded as a superior distinction, although it was actually as outmoded for use in contemporary society as the Latin language had become in the West centuries before.

Although the educated class could use the script—some of them not too well in practice—the average Turk in the city and the peasantry of the country were unable to either read or write the Turkish language in the ornate script, with its hundreds of letter forms as contrasted with the twenty-six letters in the Latin alphabet.

The religious men—the hojas and other holy men—were well versed in the script. This gave them a special advantage as interpreters not only of Islamic law and the Koran but, in many cases, of all printed matter that came to the villages.

All of this led the Ghazi to abolish the Caliph's decree, which had been in force since 1723.

The Ghazi's orders, in 1931, made it obligatory to print the Koran in the Turkish language, and rewrite all prayers into Turkish.

This led to another important step in reform. One of the Ghazi's long-range programs concerned the revision of the Turkish alphabet itself and a purification of the language.

The adoption of Arabic script as the written form of the Turkish language had inhibited the language, for the script was incongruous with Turkish. The Semitic Arabic characters or letters were not suited to the sounds of Turkish. One example of the incongruity was the fact that the Turkish language, which is Ural-Altaic in origin, has many vowels while Arabic has few.

This difficulty, as well as others, made learning to read and write Turkish in Arabic a very arduous task requiring years of study. Arabic was used by most educated Turks rather than Turkish, producing a huge gap between the language spoken by the mass of the people and that used by those of learning.

Another problem in the use of the Arabic script was the fact that, despite centuries of use, the Arabic vocabulary had not really progressed. It had become largely an academic or dead language. While many new words

149

were injected into the language, even as early as the last Ottoman regime during World War I, little progress in modernizing the language had been made.

"The needs of the Turkish language are clear," Kemal exclaimed as he urged the reform of the alphabet and the acceptance of the Latin alphabet in place of Arabic script.

"These letters," he said, "have been accepted by many nations and have become a means of sharing a common culture, and since our nation wants to strengthen its connection with Western civilization, it would be profitable to adopt the Latin alphabet."

He was not the first to espouse this reform. Turkish scholars had long recognized the need to update and adjust the language.

In 1926, in fact, the Turkish-speaking minorities of the Soviet Republic had called a Turkeological Congress, to which a Turkish delegation was invited, to study the matter. The congress met at Baku and discussed the desirability of abandoning Arabic script as "unscientific and detrimental to the Turkish language."

Mustafa Kemal heartily agreed with this, but felt that more time and study was needed before bringing the matter for a vote before the Grand National Assembly. After all, the Arabic script and all its religious implications were yet another vital nerve of the traditionalists in Turkish society, who naturally opposed language reform. They wished to perpetuate an elite class of citizens and religious persons who alone could comfortably use the more exclusive Arabic script.

Basically the same element had opposed compulsory national education for all.

The Ghazi, who felt that the archaic Arabic script was holding the Turks back in their attempts to modernize their society, was a master politician. While the difficult script did contribute to the fact that the majority of his Turks could not read or write, he wanted to wait until the time was exactly right before pushing this new reform.

In late 1927, he felt strong enough to begin preparations for his great new alphabet reform. Plans were drawn during the winter of 1928, and a great deal of investigation and research was undertaken.

Kemal knew the reform had to come soon. He believed fervently from the first that adapting Turkish to the simpler Latin alphabet would bridge yet another gap between East and West vis-à-vis Turkey. And, after all, that was the important point in the long run.

"In one year, perhaps in two, the entire Turkish social organization will learn the new letters," he boasted secretly to friends. "And our nation will show by its writing and by its intelligence that it is by the side of the whole civilized world," he added.

He finally appointed a committee to study the question. Although he knew the Turkish language contained some sounds which could not be adapted readily to the

Latin alphabet, the Ghazi was adamant. "Turkish can be adapted to the Latin alphabet," he insisted to his committee.

The Ghazi's patience was wearing thin as the winter months dragged on into spring. Many of the scholars appointed to the task of the reform, inordinately patient men, were convinced that it would take years before the proper adaptions could be made.

One had the impertinence to suggest sixteen years!

To this the Ghazi, a born teacher, who was certain that modifications, additions and adaptions could be made, would not agree.

An enormous amount of man-hours went into the Ghazi's study—not only by the appointed committee but also by independent volunteers whom Kemal rounded up from among his wide acquaintance. Poets, men of letters and even deputies in the Assembly with a knowledge of linguistics labored at the problem to please the Ghazi. Prime Minister Izmet closely followed the work and was present at most of the official committee meetings, so important was the reform program. All carefully examined the rules of Turkish grammar, syntax and orthology, and laboriously compared it with other languages.

The time dragged on.

Finally the Ghazi, always in a hurry, became even more impatient, though he grudgingly admitted that much progress had been made by the committee.

It was not enough. He set himself up as a committee

of one to see to it that the reform of the language and alphabet met a deadline of six weeks. He even set up the date on which he would unveil the new alphabet. The language, shorn of its Arabic and foreign words and in its new Latin alphabet, would be presented to a gathering of his People's Party at Seraglio Point in Istanbul on August 9, 1928.

Kemal worked feverishly with a chosen few to make ready his new project for his Turks.

The night of August 9 finally arrived, and with it the Ghazi's new alphabet.

"Friends," he told an audience sitting in the mild, balmy breeze-swept park on the banks of the Bosporus, "we are accepting new Turkish letters.

"For centuries we have had our heads in an iron circle," he went on. "Now we must free ourselves from unintelligible and uncomprehensible signs, and with these new letters we shall understand it perfectly and quickly."

"I am sure of this and you, too, may be sure of this," he said with confidence and pride.

He then dramatically undraped a simple blackboard for his audience on which the Latin alphabet was neatly printed.

"Teach every citizen—every woman, man, porter, boatman," he implored. "This is a patriotic duty.

"It is a disgrace, if only 10 to 20 per cent know how to read and write and 80 per cent do not," he added. "This nation is a nation made to feel pride; its history is filled with pride."

His great enthusiasm carried over to the crowds sitting and watching and listening to their beloved leader, but his great experiment in forcing the new alphabet would be tried before a glittering audience of politicians, diplomats and statesmen in the sugar-white Dolma Bache palace.

Here in the grand ballroom—done in marble, gilt and precious stones and illuminated by crystal chandeliers, whose lights danced upon the faces of the guests—the Ghazi staged his program.

With great drama, he arranged his presentation under the huge central chandelier that glistened with a thousand lights. The chandelier, which had been the gift of Queen Victoria of England to the Sublime Porte Sultans of the Ottoman Empire, was a fitting spotlight. England had been one of the first Western nations to extend a friendly hand to Turkey.

Each member of the distinguished audience sitting in small gilt chairs in the palace ballroom on that day, August 25, was handed printed copies of the Turkish Latinized alphabet.

At the head of the "class" stood the Ghazi, in morning clothes, before a draped object which when unveiled revealed again the simple schoolroom blackboard he would make famous as he traveled across Turkey personally instructing his countrymen in the new letters.

"This is an 'A,'" he said as he raised his teacher's pointer to the letters on the blackboard.

"Our fellow countrymen will learn the letters quickly," he said as he went down the list.

Following the demonstration and lecture, the guests were led to the wings alongside the ballroom under the old grilled harem galleries to taste the sweets and canapés prepared for them.

Kemal strode among his guests, talking of nothing but the new alphabet. It was as though affairs of state were meaningless beside the great importance of teaching his countrymen to read and write.

The Turkish press reported enthusiastically on the new alphabet, and within a few weeks the newspapers of Istanbul and the *National Sovereignty* in Angora began to print their copy in the new letters.

Kemal then took his blackboard to his capital, Angora, and had it set up in the halls of the Grand National Assembly so that he could personally introduce the new alphabet to the deputies.

"It is the key which will enable all of the people of Turkey to read and write easily," he explained as he called several deputies to the podium and requested them to demonstrate their abilities in the new alphabet.

Blackboards were then set up throughout the nation —in bazaars and simple village squares—and all were requested to learn the new letters.

No one was exempt.

So forceful was the program and so pleased was Kemal with the progress of his countrymen that he devoted the major part of his opening speech at the Grand National Assembly that fall to the establishment of the new letters.

He spoke to the deputies of the necessity of granting legal form to the adoption of the new alphabet. "It is the will of the nation," he said.

The Assembly promptly elected a committee to prepare a bill such as the Ghazi requested.

On November 3, 1928, less than three months after its first introduction to the Turkish people, the new alphabet became law and Arabic script was abandoned.

Kemal then set out to reform Turkish current history and geographic names.

By 1930 all Turkish geographic names were re-recorded in Turkish and in the new Latin alphabet.

Constantinople officially became Istanbul, Smyrna became Izmir and Angora, Turkey's new capital, was renamed Ankara.

The British Foreign Office reacted in a typically superior but amusing British fashion, continuing to address all dispatches to Angora, Turkey!

Said Winston Churchill, in an indignant moment: "Whoever heard of an Ankara cat or an Ankara rabbit?"

It was at this time, too, that a law was passed at Kemal's insistence, requiring all Turkish citizens to select a surname.

The Grand National Assembly bestowed the name Atatürk ("father of the Turks") upon Mustafa Kemal.

From that moment on, he would proudly sign his name Mustafa Kemal Atatürk or, more simply, Atatürk.

Culturally and historically, Atatürk had one more important reform remaining—to draw attention to the historical field that explained the civilized structure and development of the Turkish nation throughout time.

Atatürk was determined to wrench Turkish history and culture away from identification merely with deeds of great Islamic acts and their warriors and conquerors.

Atatürk believed that since Turkey's acceptance of Islam, the great deeds of the Turks had not been given their due. He had a great sense of history and was convinced that a belief in the historical background of a people held the greatest key for their belief in themselves. He was determined that the Turkish people should believe in their greatness—past and future!

Turkish history during the Ottoman period had gone through three stages of development.

The first stage was the period lasting from the foundation of the Ottoman state up to the time of Sultan Abdulmecid in 1839. During this entire period, only Islamic history and great Islamic deeds were considered by scholars. No place was given to the part the Turks themselves had played in the development and emergence of Islam.

The second stage was the period from the reform years after 1839 (under Abdulmecid) to the autocratic

157

regime of Abdullah. In this period some state schools had been established, and their curriculum included some secular Ottoman history. But again, no true history of the Turk was developed or allowed to flourish.

The third period, during Atatürk's lifetime, had seen a movement to establish some semblance of a national Turkish history. Many of the intellectuals during these years and up to World War I had studied abroad and had come to believe in the importance of instilling a sense of national worth in a people. But the state refused to adopt a Turkish view of history, preferring instead the traditional, religion-dominated Islamic-Ottoman view of the history of the Empire.

Atatürk, whose own sense of history was keen and highly developed, felt that his fellow Turks should be accorded a true identification that would make them proud of their native land—and proud of themselves.

"Ben olecegin" ("I am a Turk") needed to be the credo of the Turks to give them the confidence and national faith necessary for survival and progress.

He then set out on a long crusade to explain to his people—and to the outside world—that the Turks were not mere destroyers and soldiers but had established great ancient civilizations, and were the true owners of the land they tilled.

His greatest task was to inculcate within his brother Turks the national faith and sense of historic worth that were essential if the Republic was to prosper.

The year was 1931.

14

Turkey Modernizes

When Atatürk spoke of civilization, which he often did, he meant not only moral, technical and material progress for Turkey but also, as those who knew him well would later explain, civilization as the sum of the successes and advances man could achieve.

To carry out his plans, he often prodded his countrymen, using his famous technique in questioning the doubters he encountered everywhere among the conservative educated Turks:

"Which nation that desires to enter civilization has not turned to the West?" he would ask with great patience for a man in such a hurry for reform.

"We cannot shut our eyes and suppose that we live alone. We cannot put a fence around our country and live without connection with the outside world."

His first efforts included the establishment of a library for the study of true Turkish history and the establishment, in 1931, of a scholarly historical research group to examine books dealing with the subject. This first research team prepared an outline of Turkish history to briefly summarize and explain the place of the Turkish nation in the history of the world.

Atatürk advised his committee of scholars, the Turkish Historical Research Committee: "Our ancestors who founded great states were the possessors of great and comprehensive civilizations. Therefore, it is our duty to make research investigation into these. When the Turkish child recognizes the deeds of his ancestors, he will find in himself the strength for still greater deeds."

With typical enthusiasm, Atatürk himself organized a work project to investigate the background of the Turks.

He attacked the heart of the problem by asking the scholars enrolled in the project some basic questions he wanted answered.

"Who were the most ancient people of Turkey?" he asked. "And how and by whom was the first civilization established in Turkey?"

He then prodded his project committee to a more expansive view of the problem. "What was the place and service of the Turks in world history and in the civilization of the earth?"

Atatürk did not neglect the religious background of his people and their homeland, for one of the questions he posed concerned the thorough re-examination of what the true nature of Islamic history had been. "What was the place and part of the Turks in Islamic history?" he asked.

For to Atatürk this was truly the heart of instilling that sense of national worth into his Turks that he deemed so necessary to their progress as a "civilized" nation.

As a result of the historical project, a four-volume general history series was produced for use in Turkish schools.

"The history of the Turkish nation is not, as it has been considered up to now, simply Ottoman history," Atatürk insisted. "The history of the Turk is very much older and has influenced the civilizations of the nations with which it has come into contact."

To further instill in the Turkish nation a sense of its historical and cultural heritage and an appreciation of its destiny, Atatürk pushed forward with the building and beautification of his new all-Turkish capital, Ankara, in the heart of the Anatolian mainland.

Ankara, where the armies of many conquering nations had trod since time immemorial, had stubbornly clung to its peculiarly Turkish flavor. A vast building program of highways and public and private buildings had changed it greatly from the tiny village clinging to its crumbling citadel, around which rude huts were clustered when the Kemalist rebels first arrived in 1920.

In 1923, when it became the capital of the then infant

161

Republic of Turkey, it had still been only a provincial town of about thirty thousand people. But by 1933, under the loving direction of Atatürk, it had become a sparkling modern city with wide, tree-lined boulevards.

Despite its most splendid expression of modern Turkey, the city also reflects the long cultural heritage of the Turks which Atatürk so desperately wanted to reinstate.

The exact date of the founding of Ankara is not known, but it is said to have been founded by the ancient Phyrigians in the eighth century B.C., though unmistakable evidence discovered recently concerning the Hittite civilization on the site indicates that it is much older.

The Lydians, the Persians and Alexander the Great's Greek Army passed this way. The town was subsequently captured by the Galatians and then the Romans. The ruins of a temple to the Emperor Augustus still stand. Later, when the Roman Empire was divided, the city came under the Byzantine Empire and, following the Crusades, under the Seljuk and then the Ottoman Turks. The famous Battle of Ankara in 1402 was fought on the plains outside the city between the Turkish Sultan Bayezit and Tamburlaine, halting the Mongol Emperor's westward march.

Modern as the city became under Atatürk, many of the old ways persisted. Peddlers can still be seen jingling musical camel bells as they balance a yoke across their humped shoulders from which bowls of yogurt for sale are strung. Donkeys can be seen and heard as they clatter by with high mounds of hay on their small backs. Peasant women in long black skirts and shawls follow behind, brandishing switches.

On the steep streets just outside the ancient citadel are open-air bazaars where copper and brass items are sold. Within the labyrinth of the citadel itself, coppersmiths can be seen at work beside outdoor fires as they copper-plate tin vessels to be offered for sale in the bazaars.

So much of the old remains alongside the new even today in Turkey's capital city. It is a profound reminder of the quick march into the twentieth century that the nation accomplished under the leadership of Atatürk. The contrasting scenes are also a poignant reminder of the struggle Turkey has undergone to become a modern nation.

Along with other modernization Atatürk set in motion vast industrial and business reforms. In order to progress, Turkey's basic economy had to be shaken to its foundations. Prior to 1927 there were few factories within the nation. Turkey's peasants or farmers produced raw material, such as cotton. But it was shipped to England, where it was made into cloth which Turkey in return repurchased.

Atatürk wanted Turkey to have her own industries. A law was passed in the National Assembly under which the government provided capital and land for the building of manufacturing and processing plants to free the Turkish economy from foreign domination.

Atatürk believed that the collapse of the Ottoman Empire was rooted in the fact that the state had not become an economic power. The Empire had, in fact, become simply a market for the developing industry of Europe. He felt that the new Turkish Republic should heed the lessons of the past.

"However great are political and military triumphs, unless those victories are crowned by economic victory they cannot last and they will fade in a short time," he warned his countrymen as he pushed the nation forward into a closer understanding of economic problems and solutions.

As virtual dictator of Turkey, Atatürk was able to arrange to have the government adjust and control the economy in order that the greatest benefits for the greatest number of people could be attained.

He would eulogize the Turkish peasant in his best Socratic style before the National Assembly.

"Give me leave to ask a question of the noble Assembly and of the whole world. Who is the Lord and Master of Turkey?

"Let me give the answer to this at once. The real Lord and Master of Turkey is the peasant, who is the producer. This being so, the peasant deserves the most prosperity, happiness and wealth."

He made a concentrated effort to destroy a set of detrimental notions that had encouraged indifference towards the peasants by the more enlightened in the nation and by the intellectuals for centuries.

"Let us adopt an attitude of respect in the presence of

this real master," he would plead, "whose blood we have shed, sending him through seven centuries to various parts of the world, whose bones we have left in foreign lands, whose labor we have taken and used.

"And in return we have repaid him with contempt and humiliation, . . . reducing him to the condition of a servant."

To transform the peasant from the landless, almost serflike worker on absentee farm holdings, Atatürk encouraged the development of farm cooperatives, distributed government land and set up *kombinats,* or farm machinery distribution centers, where the peasants could borrow the tools they needed for more productive farming.

Mustafa Kemal Atatürk also sought to overthrow the idea held by his countrymen that poverty was a virtue.

"Let us put an end to the philosophy that supposes complacency an inexhaustible treasure and knows poverty as virtue," he insisted.

To further bolster the new philosophy of the dignity of the farmer, he organized an experimental model farm on his Chakaya estate outside Ankara. Here Atatürk, the President of the land, could be seen working the soil and driving his tractor. He often discussed farm problems that he himself encountered as he worked with other local farmers.

By doing as well as preaching, Atatürk felt he could raise the peasantry to a position of dignity and make all Turkey realize the importance of the men of the soil, who were, after all, the majority in the land and those upon whom the country so depended.

His greatest accolade was a tribute he made in these words: "The arm that wields the sword tires, but the arm that guides the plow grows stronger every day."

One other area of vast importance in raising Turkey's standard of living was a careful analysis of the state's economic and budgetary problems.

These were vast. A very large part of the sources of wealth in the nation had been destroyed in the Turco-Greek war. Both home markets and foreign trade had been disrupted, and while concessions to foreign business were discouraged, foreign capital was needed.

The press began to criticize, in a limited way, the government's attitude, pointing out the paucity of capital within Turkey and suggesting the need to encourage rather than discourage foreign enterprise and money to aid the sagging Turkish economy.

To counteract such criticism, Atatürk immediately issued a statement as to the government's true role.

"In order to render our country prosperous in a short time, and in view of the inadequacy of the capital of the nation, it is necessary that we make use of foreign capital.

"So let it not be thought that we are opposed to foreign capital. Therefore, on condition that it respects the law, we are welcoming foreign effort and means."

He emphasized the importance of cooperation within the established laws of the land to dispel any question in any Turk's mind that this meant a return to Ottoman policies of concessions.

To bring about an economic rebirth of the nation, Atatürk then introduced an economic plan which would attack the problem in carefully controlled stages.

State monopolies were set up with government support in numerous industries, such as weaving and the tobacco industry, both of which were so important to the national economy.

The government's economic policies followed closely the Soviet system's experiments in economic planning, closely governed by the state. For example, programs of three-, four- or five-year "plans" were developed for agriculture, mining and various industries and óther facets of the economy.

A ten-year program of road building was begun.

Also important, for a country with limited resources and revenue, was the setting up of government-controlled banks to instill confidence for investors in Turkey's economy and to aid the economic process of rehabilitation.

Atatürk followed a rigorous program of inviting trained engineers and plant managers to come to Turkey and help solve the nation's lack of skilled management and labor. He also encouraged Turkey's young scientific minds to go abroad to learn the necessary skills that would train them for the complex modern technological era he was determined Turkey would enter.

His was an "operation bootstraps" for all Turks, young and old.

There were those in the country who felt Turkey should remain an agricultural country as she had always been.

"I am opposed," Atatürk said, "to the giving of any definition that would limit the Turkish economy.

"I want the word 'economy' to be understood in the widest sense . . . , for Economy means everything. . . . It means agriculture; it means industry; it means everything."

15

Father-Turk

In the last few years of his life, Atatürk was often quite ill. He suffered painfully from a serious malady of the liver and was often confined to his room for days at a time.

Often he stayed on his yacht, the *Savarona*—moored outside the Dolma Bache palace, where he resided when in Istanbul—enjoying the refreshing breezes of the waters of the Bosporus.

"I waited for this yacht like a child expecting a toy," he explained to his close friend Ali Fuad, with whom he spent considerable time during his last years.

"If I have to stay in bed, I shall be terribly bored. I shall be able to bear it only with the help of friends like yourself," he told him.

Yet he still had important work to do.

There were serious international and internal problems to be solved. By the mid-'30s, Europe was already drifting toward war. Mussolini, dictator of Italy, invaded the ancient African kingdom of Abyssinia (Ethiopia) in 1935 and announced a grandiose scheme of aggression that he planned not only in North Africa but in Asia as well. The announcement could lead to a serious alteration in the Middle-East structure. Atatürk, a pronounced neutral, was keenly concerned.

Hitler, in Germany's Reich, would follow with a sinister remilitarization of the Rhineland the following year. These moves led Turkey to establish a series of security treaties with neighboring Balkan states and Russia and a closer rapprochement with both Great Britain and France, from whom she had been estranged since the end of World War I.

The crises of Europe, however, gave Turkey an opportunity to reopen the vexing disputes between her and Western Europe, such as the ownership and militarization of the straits of the Bosporus and the Dardanelles and the settlement of the question of the former Turkish province of Alexandretta, called the Hatay, still under foreign control.

Atatürk's ministers took advantage of the unrest in Europe to bring these matters up for discussion, and the resulting Agreement of Montreux, signed on July 30, 1936, erased the provisions of the Treaty of Lausanne concerning the status of the Straits. They were returned to Turkey, and provisions were made for Turkish military control of this important waterway between the Mediterranean and the Black Sea. All the Lausanne Treaty signatories, with the exception of Italy, accepted the reversal of the World War I agreements.

The problem of the Hatay, which Atatürk considered vital to Turkey's integrity as a sovereign state, was more difficult to resolve. According to a Franco-Syrian Treaty of September, 1936, France had agreed to the independence of Syria, formerly under her mandate. The agreement included the Hatay, with its large Turkish-speaking population. So instead of being a simple Franco-Turkish problem, the area included a third state, which, with its new nationalistic fervor, jealously looked on Turkey's claim as a threat to its newly won independence.

But since a large portion of the population of the area in dispute was Turkish—some experts reported more than 40 per cent—Atatürk was determined to peacefully fight for the province. He had his ministers present the problem before the League of Nations in Geneva, to which Turkey had been admitted in 1932.

The League took up the matter and recommended a plebiscite. The result was victory for the Turkish cause as the people went to the polls, policed by both Turkish and French authorities, and voted in favor of autonomy of the Hatay. Then, under their newly elected pro-Turkish Assembly, the Republic of the Hatay was annexed by Turkey.

"The joy felt at the national problem of the Hatay

being settled by friendly measures is well placed," Atatürk told a rejoicing Turkish populace at the news. It was a personal triumph for Atatürk, since the deliverance of the Hatay from foreign control was the culmination of a dream begun at the time of the War of Independence for a consolidated and complete Turkey for the Turks. He rejoiced in regaining this last bit of true Turkish soil.

"We want nothing but to live free and independent within our national frontiers," he would reiterate. "In our foreign policy there is no attack on the rights of any other state."

Atatürk was already astutely aware of how small the world really was and how interdependent its nations. He sought to teach his fellow countrymen this.

The idea was actually revolutionary in 1937. Even in Europe, many of the major nations did not recognize this truism or accept a one-world philosophy until after they had faced the cruel decisions forced upon them by the advent of World War II.

"Today all the nations of the world are in a way relations," he would caution.

"And in this way, as a man considers the prosperity and happiness of the nation to which he belongs, so must he consider the peace and well-being of all nations. As he values the prosperity of his own nation, so must he try to do all he can to serve the happiness of the nations of the world.

"If in the world and between the nations of the world there is no peace, whatever a nation does for itself, it has no tranquillity. And for this reason we must regard humanity as one among us," he added prophetically in one of his periodic speeches at the National Assembly.

Though critics often accused Atatürk of being intoxicated with power, it is undeniable that he strove doggedly to make the nation a healthier and more democratic place in which to live.

Turkey had indeed come a long way in the fifteen years since Atatürk had assumed control of the Turkish state. And while he ruled as a dictator—and often as a ruthless one at that—his hopes were for the future of Turkey as a free and democratic state.

To Atatürk, his one-man rule had been a necessity to rid the country of its past. Like a tree surgeon who whacks off dead branches, so had he attacked Turkey's long, autocratic past, and chopped them off one by one at the central trunk to rid the state of old and diseased parts. Through his careful and systematic pruning of the old, he had provided his Turks with a nation in the flower of new and vigorous growth.

Already he had proved to the world that Turkey had the basic right to exist as an independent state. Now he wanted to apply the concept of political rights in a personal as well as national sense.

"Every nation must have control over its own destiny.

And rights for individuals are sacred, too," he said. "These rights for individuals as for nations are a guarantee of basic existence."

But his regime was a dictatorship, and this disturbed him.

"I do not want to die without bringing the regime of personal rule in Turkey to a close," he told his friend Ali Fuad.

In defense of his assumption of dictatorial control over the Republic he could honestly boast that, because of his methods, the Republic could move forward and eventually live under a wider and more meaningful democratic process.

His eyes were not on the generation nurtured by the Revolution, but on the generation to come.

The Turkish Revolution, while a remarkable and unique experiment in the Middle East, had touched only the better-educated and the more politically enlightened. It was still only a thin veneer, not securely rooted in the hearts of the peasants who formed the majority of the population.

Atatürk was aware of this. As he traveled through the land he could read in the dark, almost expressionless eyes of the peasants and in their still passive resignation an unawareness and unconcern. It was as though they were still only timeless observers and not participants in the experiment of self-government.

Those dark eyes haunted him like empty windows in

a darkened room, and he wanted to see light there. "But how?" he wondered.

He finally came to the decision that a second party should be launched so that the people could vote for a choice of candidates, and not simply for those of the Republican People's Party he had founded and headed.

His efforts to form a second political party came as something of a bombshell. Some critics went so far as to suggest it was merely an attempt to get rid of Prime Minister Ismet Inönü.

This was far from the truth, however, for Ismet, often at odds with the Ghazi and no longer the close confidant he had been throughout the formulative years of the Republic, was held in great respect by Atatürk.

His purpose was to get true representative government for his Turks. The new party, under the leadership of Atatürk's old friend Fethi Bey, had as its main purpose the establishment of a more democratic base.

The experiment was to end in failure, however, for— unlike the American and French Revolutions, under which republics were founded—the majority of the population was not already dedicated to the proposition of liberty and equality. Turkey in the 1930s was still too politically immature for true parliamentary government and a multiparty system.

Once the new party was launched, after years of one-man rule, numerous outbreaks and even riots occurred. Fethi Bey, the personally selected head of the party, was frequently set upon by indignant Kemalists, who saw in him a rival opposed to the Republic itself. And since many dissidents and discontented politicians could be found, the party acted as a catalyst for disgruntled persons everywhere in the country.

One tragic incident occurred. A sect of religious fanatics called the Nakhshbendi, led by a dervish called Mehmet, began a march on the Turkish coast near Izmir. Everywhere they went they advocated a return to the Seriat (holy law), the wearing of the veil, the return of the fez, the readoption of Arabic script for the Turkish language and reinstallation of religion as the basis of the state.

The march enraged large groups of Kemalists and led eventually to riots, the shooting of several persons and the barbarous slaying of a Turkish Army officer.

Ultimately, about one hundred persons were arrested, martial law was proclaimed and seven of the sect were hanged to quell the riots. The government charged sedition and the attempted overthrow of the Republic.

Sadly, the Ghazi had to admit the country was not ready for democracy—not just then, at any rate. Fethi Bey dissolved the party. Led and fed by his own patriotism and enthusiasm for the common man's will, Atatürk exhibited an almost juvenile sense of devotion to model the government on Western ideals which the people were not quite ready to accept. He prematurely assumed that all of his Turks were ready for self-government.

This dream was to prove an illusion in his lifetime.

The Oriental heritage which had stretched over thousands of years could not so easily be bridged. A brilliant beginning had been made, however. When matched against the progress of democracy in the West, Atatürk's few years with his Turks would yield great benefits.

Mustafa Kemal Atatürk had indeed "fathered" a modern Turkey. At his death, on November 10, 1938, he could indeed take pride in having been a Turk and in having founded a republic that would live on after his death.

He had led his people by the hand along the path of democracy until their feet were steadied and they knew the direction they must take.

"Their children will surely be free," he said.

Following the Ghazi's death in the early hours of that gray November morning, the Assembly convened and promptly elected Ismet Inönü President. Dedicated to the Kemalist reforms and dreams for Turkey, he would lead the nation forward along the guidelines Atatürk had established.

"The Republican People's Party will carry out the wishes of the Eternal Chief," he told the delegates.

After World War II, Inönü felt a new experiment in a two-party system was feasible and helped form a second party, which was called the Democratic Party.

This time the second party was successfully launched, and in 1950 the Democrats won the election for the Presidency. The experiment in two-party rule was not an immediate success, however, as the new party leaders placed Atatürk's old Republican People's Party under a ban and reintroduced censorship of the press. The Democrats were in turn overthrown in 1960 by a military coup.

Since 1960 Turkey has again experimented in two-party parliamentary procedures with elections as spirited as Atatürk would have wished.

"I want to create a true Republic," he had once said. And he had.

The reformist spirit Atatürk had generated in his lifetime lived on after his death. His legacy to the nation was a healthier and more democratic sharing of powers between his successors—a rare inheritance from a dictator.

Now all his Turks can proudly say, *"Ben olecegan"* with true meaning.

Atatürk had shown the way.

The Treaty of Sêvres

August 20, 1920: The feeble, dying government of the last Ottoman Sultan (Mohammed VI) of Turkey signed the Treaty of Sêvres at San Remo, Italy.

1. Territorial Provisions:

By this treaty the Sultan's government renounced all claim to non-Turkish territory.

A. Turkey was shorn of all Arab lands in her Empire. The kingdom of Hejaz became an independent state, and Turkey renounced control of Syria, Palestine and Mesopotamia, whose destinies were placed under international mandates of the Allied Powers—Syria to France and the latter two mandates to Great Britain.

B. Smyrna and the Aegean Islands were placed under Greek administration. Smyrna was to be permitted a plebiscite, by request of the population, after five years under Greek control. The Dodecanese Islands, including the island of Rhodes, were excepted and ceded to Italy under the terms of the treaty.

C. Armenia was recognized as an independent state, with the boundaries between Turkey and Armenia to

179

be arbitrated according to provisions supplied the Allies by President Woodrow Wilson of the United States.*

D. Certain Kurdish territories east of the Euphrates were to be granted autonomy under provisions to be set up under an International Commission composed of French, British and Italian representatives. Turkey also agreed to boundary modification concerning Kurdish lands in the area of the frontier between her and Iran.

E. Eastern Thrace was ceded to Greece up to the Chatalja line. Western Thrace, previously ceded to Greece by defeated Bulgaria, was granted to Greece by the Allies.

F. The Straits and Constantinople were to remain in Turkey's possession, subject to strict Allied control. The Straits were to be demilitarized and placed under international control. The capitulations, under which foreigners residing in Turkey were accorded special privileges outside Turkish jurisdiction, were to be continued.

G. The Turkish Army was to be limited to 50,000 men, compulsory military service was to be abolished and

* The provisions of the Treaty of Sèvres were never recognized by the Kemalist government. Following a Turco-Armenian peace treaty arranged in December, 1920, Armenia became a republic of the U.S.S.R. with the exception of the Turkish provinces of Kars and Ardahan.

a limit was placed on Turkish armament.

H. A financial commission of Allied (French, British and Italian) representatives were to have control of and supervision over the nation's budget, debts, customs and indirect taxes.

The Treaty of Lausanne

July 24, 1923: The Turkish Nationalists (Mustafa Kemal's government) signed the Treaty of Lausanne, under which Turkey regained her independence and many of the more odious conditions imposed by the Treaty of Sèvres were rescinded.

1. Territorial Provisions:

Under the provisions of the treaty, the Kemalists obtained recognition of the new Turkish state and buried the remnants of the Ottoman regimes.

A. Turkey gave up all claims to non-Turkish territory. She recovered Eastern Thrace to the Maritza River and regained the islands of Imbros (which guards the Straits) and Tenedos. The rest of the Aegean Islands were ceded to Greece; Italy retained the Dodecanese and England Cypress.

B. The capitulations were abolished.

C. Turkey regained the Straits, which were to remain demilitarized with provisions that they be opened to all nations in time of peace and in time of war *if* Turkey remained neutral. *If* Turkey was at war, enemy ships were allowed to be excluded, but not those of neutral nations.

D. The boundary with Syria was to be defined as that of the Franklin-Bouillon Agreements of October 20, 1921, which, except for the province of the Hatay, Alexandretta, is Turkey's southern border today. The independence of Armenia and the independence or autonomy of Kurdistan were not mentioned in the provisions of the treaty. The boundary with Iraq was left for future negotiations between sovereign Turkey and Great Britain, which retained its mandate over that Arab land.

E. The evacuation of Constantinople by the Allies was agreed upon.

2. A separate Turco-Greek agreement was arranged for the compulsory exchange of populations, though Greeks living in Constantinople and Turks living in Thrace were excluded from the agreements.

BIBLIOGRAPHY

Armstrong, Harold C. *The Grey Wolf.* New York: Minton, 1933.

Atatürk, Mustafa Kemal. *Speech.* Istanbul: Turkish Ministry of Education, 1927.

Bridge, Anne. *The Dark Moment.* New York: MacMillan, 1952.

Brock, Ray. *Ghost On Horseback.* New York: Duell, Sloan & Pearce, 1954.

Churchill, Winston S. *The World Crises,* (6 vols.) New York: Charles Scribner's Sons, 1923-31.

Grew, Joseph C. *Turbulent Era: A Diplomatic Record of Forty Years, 1904-1945* (2 vols., Walter Johnson, ed.) Freeport, N.Y.: Books for Libraries, Inc., 1952.

Grolier Society. *The Changing Face of Turkey.* (Lands and Peoples Series) New York: 1938.

Kinross, Lord. *Atatürk: A Biography of Mustafa Kemal, Father of Modern Turkey.* New York: William Morrow & Co., Inc., 1966.

————. *Within the Taurus.* New York: William Morrow & Co., Inc., 1955.

Langer, William L., ed. *Encyclopedia of World History.* Boston: Houghton Mifflin Co., 1968.

Lenczowski, George. *The Middle East in World Affairs.* Ithaca, N.Y.: Cornell University Press, 1962.

184

Lengyel, Emil. *They Called Him Atatürk.* New York: John Day Co., 1962.

Moorehead, Alan. *Gallipoli.* New York: Harper & Row, 1956.

Muller, H. J. *The Loom of History.* New York: Harper & Row, 1958.

Turkish Ministry of Press Broadcasting & Tourism. *Atatürk.* Ankara: 1961.

Turkish Ministry of Tourism & Information. *Turkey.* Istanbul: 1967.

Turkish Tourism and Information Office. *Film Clips on the Life of Atatürk.* New York.

Walker, Warren S. and Uysal, Ahmet E. *Tales Alive in Turkey.* Cambridge, Mass.: Harvard University Press, 1966.

INDEX

187

188

Index

ABOUT THE AUTHOR

Deane Fons Heller was born in Milwaukee, Wisconsin. She attended the University of Chicago and the University of Maryland at College Park, and was a reporter for the Chicago *Sun* before becoming a free lance writer of political and travel features. For many years, she was a correspondent for Central Press of King Features and a special writer for the *Washington Star Magazine* in Washington, D.C., where she made her home for twenty years with her late husband and collaborator, David Heller.

More recently, she has been a special writer for the *Miami Herald*. She is the author of several thousand magazine and newspaper feature and travel articles for a wide range of publications, including *The New York Times*, the *Christian Science Monitor* and the *Washington Post*. She was one of the four charter incorporators and the first woman member of the Society of American Travel Writers, was selected for inclusion in *American Women in Communications* in 1970 and was nominated to the distinguished British society, 2000 Women of Achievement, in 1971–72. She has two sons— David, a Vietnam veteran and graduate of the Couers de Civilization, the Sorbonne and George Washington University, and Douglas, a student at the Baylor School, Chattanooga, Tenn. She is the wife of James L. Erickson, a U.S. Naval Supply Corp. officer, and makes her home in Key West, Florida.